CONTENTS

Opposite: Sunset at St Ronan's Bay.

Above: An aerial view of the island from the south.

HIGHLIGHTS

Iona is a small island, and can easily be explored in two or three days. If you are here for a day or less, you may wish to spend that time exploring the historic monuments of the abbey and the surrounding area. Here are our recommendations.

THE ABBEY

▶ THE HIGH CROSSES

Three tall, ornately carved crosses, dating from the 700s and 800s, once stood in front of the abbey church, with a fourth in the Reilig Odhrain graveyard. St Martin's has stood in its original position for more than 12 centuries, and a replica of St John's Cross can be seen just outside the abbey church (p.8).

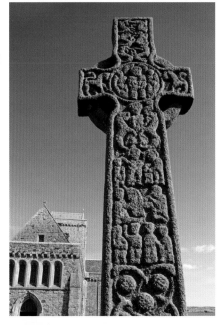

▲ THE CROSSING

The centre of the abbey church, directly below the tower, dates mostly from the 1400s, though traces of the first Benedictine church of 1200–20 still survive. The columns feature intricate carvings from biblical and everyday life and include the signature of the master mason. The north transept has a display which tells the story of the life of St Columba (p.18).

◀ THE CHAPTER HOUSE

The place where the monks gathered for daily meetings. The original stone seating survives around the walls of the inner chamber, with a display telling the story of the Iona Community in the outer (p.25).

▲ THE CLOISTER

Although largely reconstructed in the 1950s, the arcaded walkways surrounding the central garden remain much as they were in the days of the Benedictine abbey – though they would then have been decorated in bright colours. Many of the graveslabs commemorating the West Highland nobility are now displayed around the cloister (p.24).

◀ THE IONA ABBEY MUSEUM – IONA ACROSS TIME

The museum tells the story of Iona and features the finest collection of early medieval carved stone crosses in Scotland, the chief surviving evidence of Columba's monastery. Other exhibits focus on the later medieval Benedictine monastery and how Iona developed as a place of pilgrimage (p.27).

◀ MACLEAN'S CROSS

Tall, ornately carved and extremely slender, MacLean's Cross has survived almost intact since it was erected around 1500, by a chief of the powerful Clan MacLean of Mull. Positioned on the pilgrimage route to Columba's shrine, it would have served as a focus for prayer (p.40).

◀ ST ORAN'S CHAPEL

A small chapel built in the 1100s, probably by Somerled, King of the Isles, or by his son Ranald, as a dynastic burial place (p.39).

▼ THE MARBLE QUARRY

A relic from an ill-fated venture of the late 1700s to capitalise on the island's seam of marble. The quarry lies in a bay in the south-east of the island and is accessible on foot. Some of the machinery still survives at the site (p.46).

◀ IONA HERITAGE CENTRE

Beside the parish church is the manse, built in 1828 to house the minister. The ground floor now serves as the Iona Heritage Centre, drawing on old photographs, newspaper archives and local memory to focus on the islanders' story – their crofting way of life, schooling and leisure, trades, customs and crafts. There are also displays on Iona's geology, natural history and Celtic art (p.41).

▼ THE NUNNERY

Established around 1200, in tandem with the Benedictine abbey, the Augustinian nunnery is now a very attractive ruin. Much of the church and its small north chapel survive, as do parts of its cloister buildings (p.42).

▼ COLUMBA'S BAY

The pretty bay known as Port a' Churaich at the southern tip of the island, where Columba is said to have made landfall when he first arrived here. A fairly long walk is rewarded with a view across the Irish Sea toward the saint's homeland (p.46).

IONA ABBEY AT A GLANCE

Most of the buildings of the Benedictine abbey have been restored or rebuilt during the last 100 years, but they are laid out much as they would have been in the early 1200s. Incredibly, important parts of the much earlier Columban monastery can still be seen. These are the main features.

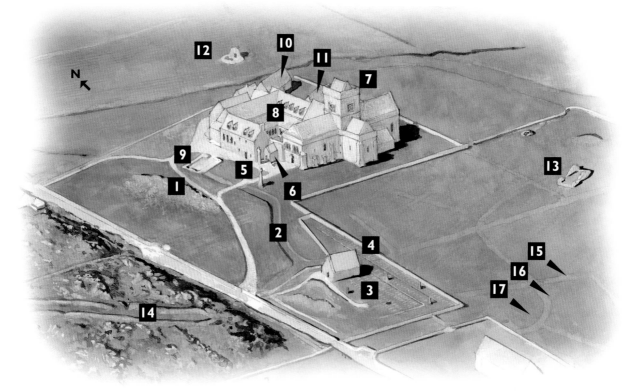

1 TÒRR AN ABA ('HILL OF THE ABBOT')
This little rocky knoll may have been the site of Columba's writing hut. A socket for a later standing cross survives on its summit.

2 SRÀID NAM MARBH ('STREET OF THE DEAD')
A processional road dating from the 700s which led the faithful past the high crosses to the holy-of-holies, St Columba's shrine.

3 REILIG ODHRAIN ('ORAN'S BURIAL GROUND')
This graveyard originated as the monastic burial ground, but from the 1100s it was the burial place of the clans, loyal to their MacDonald lords in death as well as in life.

4 ST ORAN'S CHAPEL
This peaceful little chapel shelters the bones of the greatest warrior leaders of the West Highlands, here in the sacred soil of Iona.

5 ST MARTIN'S CROSS AND ST JOHN'S CROSS
The grouping of high crosses proclaimed the location of St Columba's Shrine. Their carved decoration helped the monks to explore the divinity of Christ, as scripture in stone.

6 ST COLUMBA'S SHRINE
This small stone building, originally freestanding, is thought to have been built over Columba's grave when it was opened around 750. It became the ultimate goal for countless generations of pilgrims.

7 CHURCH OF THE CLANS
A church has stood on this site for almost 1,500 years, the latest being the church of the Benedictine monastery, which was begun around 1200, reinvigorating religious life at Iona. This was the largest church in the West Highlands and islands.

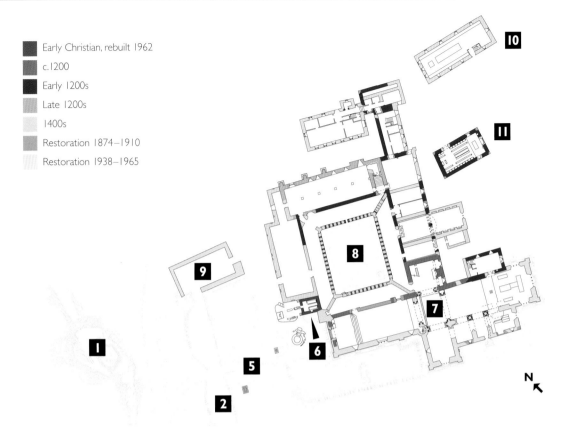

Early Christian, rebuilt 1962
c.1200
Early 1200s
Late 1200s
1400s
Restoration 1874–1910
Restoration 1938–1965

8 CLOISTER
The monks spent most of their daily lives in the buildings around this central court. The covered alleys linked the domestic accommodation with the church and provided a place for quiet contemplation.

9 BAKEHOUSE
Set apart from the abbey due to fire risk, this helped to supply the monastic community with food.

10 ABBEY MUSEUM – *IONA ACROSS TIME*
This restored building, which probably once served as the monks' hospital, now houses the finest collection of early Christian carved stone crosses in Britain and Ireland.

11 MICHAEL CHAPEL
This small chapel formed part of the abbey in the early 1200s, perhaps serving as a temporary place of worship while the church was being built.

12 TAIGH AN EASBUIG ('BISHOP'S HOUSE')
A remnant of the residence built for the bishop, probably in the 1630s, when the abbey briefly became the Cathedral of the Isles.

13 ST MARY'S CHAPEL
A tiny ruined chapel, probably dating from the 1200s, and likely to have been one of a number of pilgrimage stations around the shrine of St Columba.

14 VALLUM
A pair of earth banks, with a deep ditch between them, which marked the boundary of Columba's monastery. Parts of the vallum were constructed for a settlement enclosure in the Iron Age, about 600 years before Columba arrived here.

15 NUNNERY
Although ruined, this Augustinian nunnery, established around 1200, is one of the best preserved in Britain.

16 TEAMPULL RÒNAIN (ST RONAN'S CHAPEL)
Close to the nunnery, this little chapel was the parish church for the islanders from around 1200 until the Reformation of the 1500s.

17 MacLEAN'S CROSS
Erected in the late 1400s, this slender prayer cross marks the point where Sràid nam Marbh meets the track leading from the landing place. Pilgrims may have paused here to pray as part of the pilgrimage route around the island.

TÒRR AN ABA ('HILL OF THE ABBOT')

The little rocky knoll to your left as you enter the abbey grounds is a good place from which to view the abbey complex. Columba is believed to have had his writing hut here, while keeping an eye on his monks.

The stone socket of a later cross can be seen on the summit of the mound, marking the special significance of this place. From this point you can follow the line of the vallum (or bank and ditch) which formed a protective enclosure around the Columban monastery.

Although much of the vallum is now lost to sight (see page 36), we know that the buildings of the Columban community lay within its boundary. They included at least one church, the saint's shrine, accommodation for monks, guests and pilgrims and many of the domestic, agricultural and industrial buildings which served the community.

We know little of the layout of these buildings, although it is likely that from earliest times the church occupied the same site.

From here, to your right, you can also see the burial ground, Reilig Odhrain, where many early Christian graveslabs were found, and St Oran's Chapel, built in the 1100s.

Above: Tòrr an Aba, with the abbey church beyond.

SRÀID NAM MARBH ('STREET OF THE DEAD')

This cobbled track, constructed of red Mull granite, is the remnant of a road which began at the Port nam Mairtear ('Martyrs' Bay') beyond the present pier and led the faithful through the burial ground, ending at Columba's shrine and the abbey church.

This is the only section of Sràid nam Marbh now visible. It runs to the ruined bakehouse, but in the past the main road, no longer visible, led directly to the abbey.

The street originated as a processional way central to the worship of Columba's monks, but its stones were later polished by the feet of countless pilgrims. It was along this track that the bodies of great Gaelic lords were carried before burial in St Oran's chapel.

Above: Sràid nam Marbh, leading towards the abbey.

THE HIGH CROSSES

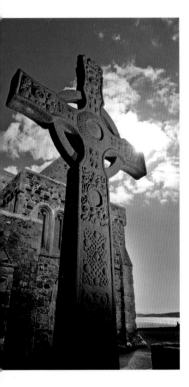

Three ornately carved high crosses once stood between Sràid nam Marbh and the abbey church, with a fourth in Reilig Odhrain. All survive, in various states of repair.

For almost 14 centuries, St Martin's Cross has stood on this spot, bearing silent witness to great events at Iona. Furthest from the church, it is the only original cross to survive intact. It was sculpted from a single stone slab imported from the Argyll mainland. The west face (facing away from the church) is carved with scenes from the Bible, while the side facing the church is richly decorated with bosses and serpents. There are slots in the ends of the short side-arms: these once held decorative mounts covered with precious metals.

The other cross outside the abbey is a modern concrete replica of St John's Cross. The original can be seen in the Abbey Museum (see page 30). With a span of almost 2.2m, it is one of the widest crosses in Britain and Ireland.

Of St Matthew's Cross only the base is still in place, while the cross itself has been re-erected in the museum. The large socketed base for St Oran's Cross can be seen on the side of the path to the east of the graveyard chapel. This high cross once marked the entrance into the graveyard, and now stands in the Abbey Museum.

All four crosses date from the 700s and 800s, and probably once formed part of a much larger group of crosses, some made of wood, which marked the pilgrims' route from their landing-place to St Columba's shrine. They would also have served as places to pause and pray.

For more information on Iona's high crosses, see pages 30–1.

Above: The replica of St John's Cross, to the west of the abbey church.

Below: The base of St Matthew's Cross. Its fragments can be seen in the infirmary museum.

DID YOU KNOW...

Early Christians worshipped facing the east, where Christ would appear on the last day. Devoted monks would face the west side of St Martin's Cross, recognising the Old Testament biblical scenes, and relating these to the central messages of Christianity – redemption and eternal life through Jesus' sacrifice on the cross.

Above: An illustration of St Oran's Cross.

Above: An illustration of St Matthew's Cross.

ST COLUMBA'S SHRINE

The little stone building to the left of the west door of the church is known as St Columba's shrine. Although only vestiges of the original building survive, it is likely that this modest chapel was built to contain the most precious possessions of the early monastery – the bones of the great St Columba.

Much of the building that stands today is from the restoration work of 1962. However, the lowest levels of stonework are original and may date back to the 700s or 800s. It is possible that this is the small church of Columcille visited by Magnus Barelegs, King of Norway, in 1098.

Once the saint's grave was opened and his bones became accessible, precious portable containers had to be created, all secured within a specially designed relic chapel. The main reliquary chest, which must have been the most richly decorated of its time, may have been designed as a smaller version of what became the most famous chapel in Scotland and Ireland. Even though these reliquaries were looted by the Vikings, possible fragments have been identified in Continental museums.

When first built, the chapel was freestanding, and it remained so even after the first Benedictine church was built.

Right: Columba's shrine as it may have looked when first built in the 700s or 800s.

Below: A shadow cast on St Columba's Shrine by the replica of St John's Cross.

THE LOVELY BONES

The bones of saints were believed to contain supernatural spiritual power – the more powerful the saint, the more effective his relics, and Columba was placed on a par with the prophets of the Bible. His biographer, Adomnán, tells of many miracles attributed to Columba in life and in death. His bones were so powerful that they were even toured around Ireland and Scotland in the later 700s to reinforce laws and to consecrate churches. Pilgrims came to Iona in great numbers to absorb Columba's holy power – to effect cures, or to ease their passage to Heaven.

THE MEDIEVAL ABBEY

The abbey's buildings were probably completed around 1450.
The simplicity we see today is in stark contrast to the richness
of the medieval interiors, especially in the church. Visitors, many
of whom would have only minimal experience of large stone
buildings, would have been left in little doubt of the power
and glory of God, and of the importance of this monastery.

Above: An illustration of the abbey around 1450,
with the chapter house and church cut away to reveal
their interiors. The church had recently undergone major
alterations, including the building of the present south
choir aisle, and widening of the nave. Ancillary buildings
had also been added or adapted.

1 ABBEY CHURCH

The present church was begun around 1200, when the Benedictine monks arrived. It was probably built on the site of the original church. By 1450, it had been altered several times, but its footprint was much as it is today. In the first half of the 1400s, the nave had been widened to the south, the south transept had been adapted and the present south choir aisle added. See pages 12–13 for further details.

2 CHAPTER HOUSE

The massive pillar and Romanesque arches date from the early 1200s, but the main space of the chapter house was rebuilt during the 1400s. Much of the medieval chapter house survives, including the stone benches, where monks would have sat during daily meetings. There was an upper chamber, which may have been a library.

3 EAST RANGE

The upper floor of the east range was probably the dormitory, where the monks slept. It was linked to the north transept by a night stair, allowing the monks direct access to the church for night-time services.

4 WEST RANGE

The present west range was built by the Iona Community in the 1950s. Although the medieval building has been lost, the cloister would have been enclosed on all four sides. The west range's upper floor may have included accommodation for guests, and perhaps for senior members of the community such as the cellarer. He would have been responsible for provisions held in stores on the ground floor.

5 NORTH RANGE

The upper floor of the north range was the refectory, where the monks gathered to eat. The projection on the north wall may have held a small pulpit from which a monk would have read to the brethren during meals.

6 ABBOT'S HOUSE

The most senior member of the community enjoyed more private and comfortable accommodation, which was linked to the cloister via the communal latrine.

7 LATRINE

The latrine, known as a reredorter, was linked to the dormitory. A drain ran underneath the building.

8 MICHAEL CHAPEL

This small chapel has probably stood since the 1200s, though its east window is later. It was fully restored in the 1950s, and its present name dates from that time.

9 INFIRMARY

The present building was completely rebuilt by the Iona Community in the 1960s. The infirmary would have been a substantial building, probably two storeys high, with its own kitchen and latrines.

10 BAKEHOUSE

This building, which survives as wall footings, has been tentatively identified as a bakehouse and brewhouse, set apart from the main cloister buildings to reduce the fire hazard. The abbey's kitchen may have stood nearby.

THE ABBEY CHURCH

The church was central to life in the abbey. It was here that the monks spent much of their day, in prayer or attending a round of eight daily services. The church also had to accommodate the many ceremonies and processions usual in a monastic community, as well as the demands of pilgrims.

1 AROUND 1200

The architecture of the Benedictine church, begun soon after 1200, had to reflect changing functions and therefore underwent many changes over the years. The building took the form of a cross. A square chancel at the head of the cross housed the high altar. The arms of the cross, known as transepts, and the central crossing provided space for the monks' choir and additional altars. The shaft of the cross formed the nave, where pilgrims worshipped.

The simplicity of this original layout may indicate the influence of the Cistercian monastic order. However, the interior decoration would have been anything but simple. This is all now lost, so we can only imagine the plastered walls, painted scenes and statues, as well as glittering altar vessels, all illuminated by the light of candles and lamps.

2 EARLY 1200s

Almost as soon as this work was complete, the first of many changes began, possibly reflecting the growing number of pilgrims visiting St Columba's shrine.

By 1250, the presbytery had been extended to the east, creating space for the choir stalls to extend beyond the crossing tower. A subterranean crypt was created beneath the high altar, to house some of Columba's relics, accessed by stairs in each of two narrow side aisles added to the north and south.

Above: The abbey church, seen from the south-east. At most abbeys, the cloister lay to the south of the church. Unusually, Iona's cloister was built on the north side.

1

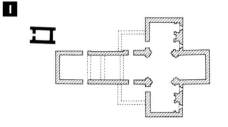

2

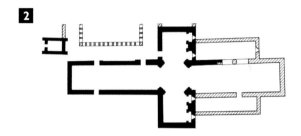

3

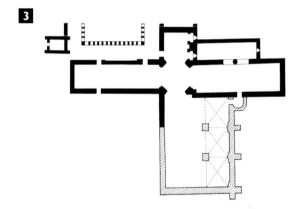

4

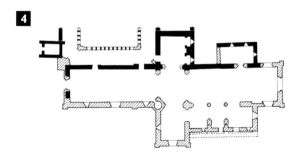

5

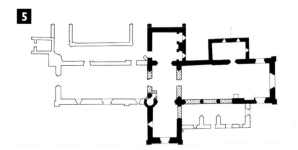

BUILDING ON THE PAST

Fragments of earlier church walls were found during rebuilding works. These showed that from the earliest days of the monastery in Columba's time, the church at its heart has always stood on this site.

Above: Workmen at the abbey during the church's reconstruction in the early 1909–10.

3 LATE 1200s

Later in the century, work began to greatly enlarge the south transept, adding three vaulted side chapels. Although this was probably never completed, its outline can still be seen in the grass to the south-east of the church.

4 MID-1400s

In the mid-1400s, the nave was widened to the south and a new west front constructed. This phase also saw the north aisle reduced in size and formed into a sacristy. The church remained like this until the abbey became derelict after the Reformation of 1560.

5 MID-1600s

An attempt in the 1630s to restore the eastern part to serve as the Cathedral of the Isles was short-lived, and restoration to its present state was not achieved until the 20th century.

Below: The head of a window in the south transept.

THE NAVE

The great processional west door gave access to the nave, a simple rectangular space without aisles, where pilgrims would have worshipped on special religious festivals. In everyday use, the monks came and went from the church via the two doorways leading north into the cloister.

The nave was extensively rebuilt in 1908–10. The upper parts of the south and west walls belong to this period, as does the distinctive five-light west window. The restoration was carried out by the architect P. MacGregor Chalmers, with funds raised largely by the Church of Scotland's Women's Guilds.

Portions of the rebuilding of the 1400s can be seen in the lower levels of the south and west walls. The upper limit of the medieval stonework is marked by a modern string course (a straight line of masonry projecting from the surface) in the west front, above the arch of the west door (itself dating to the mid-1400s). This is best seen from outside.

Other clues to the earlier arrangement also survive. An irregular scar south of the porch marks where the original south wall was demolished in the 1400s, when much of the south side of the church was rebuilt. Part of this wall is preserved under a grille south of the font, which also highlights the original floor level of the 1200s. The font itself was gifted in 1913 and is partially made of distinctive Iona marble.

The unusual change in floor level here may date from the 1400s, but there is no direct evidence for this. The north wall had been almost entirely demolished before the modern rebuilding, but the lowest levels in both doorways remain.

Above: The font, installed in 1913, is made partly from marble quarried on the island.

Opposite: Looking west along the nave, parts of which survive from the church built around 1200. Visitors are invited to attend the daily services held here.

CARVED GRAVE STONES

The stone carvings of Iona are one of the highlights of a visit to the abbey. Along the south wall of the nave there are six West Highland graveslabs, four of which bear effigies of later-medieval clerics of the abbey.

These graveslabs are part of a larger collection of medieval carved stones which is one of the abbey's treasures. Many more can be seen in the Abbey Museum, around the cloister and in St Oran's Chapel. Some were produced by sculptors based on Iona, while others were made by skilled craftsmen who travelled widely in western Scotland to work.

Left: The upright grave marker of a monk-priest, showing a ring-headed altar cross flanked by the altar vessels used during Mass: a paten (dish) and a chalice (cup).

Above: The warrior graveslab of MacKinnon chiefs of the 1300s, from St Oran's Chapel, now displayed in the museum. Eventually, five generations were buried under this slab, requiring an additional inscription on the top edge.

This distinctive body of West Highland sculpture was created between the 1200s and 1500s. The graveslabs were laid flat to cover graves in St Oran's Chapel, Reilig Odhrain and the cemetery by the nunnery. Some were lids for stone coffins, originally inside the churches, or else in the open air. They commemorate the leading members of the West Highland clans, including MacKinnons, MacLeans and MacLeods, all loyal supporters of the mighty MacDonald Lords of the Isles. While some were 'the best men of all the Isles', others were rich mercenaries, landless younger sons, who had the cash to invest in this kind of immortality.

They bear distinctive foliage-ornament and often swords, hunting scenes and other figural panels. Several also depict the distinctive Highland galley, the birlinn.

Most of the graveslabs were removed from Reilig Odhrain in the mid-1900s and placed indoors for their preservation. They had been rearranged in the mid-1800s by the Duke of Argyll, who positioned them in rows, a 'ridge of kings' and a 'ridge of chiefs', within iron railings, so it is now impossible to tell how they were originally arranged in the medieval period.

For more information on Iona's carved stones, see pages 27–33.

Below: The six carved slabs displayed in the nave. These stones once covered the graves of medieval clerics in Reilig Odhrain. Four of them feature effigies of the holy men they commemorate.

REINVENTING THE MɑCDONALD DYNASTY

At least two slabs may have been adapted or newly created to commemorate great ancestral heroes of the MacDonald Lords of the Isles, whose original memorials were lost, as part of the process of creating a regal aura around their lordship. Both these slabs would have been inside St Oran's Chapel.

One of the slabs (below left) could be associated with King Ranald, son of Somerled (Ragnall mac Somairle), who founded the Benedictine abbey around 1200. It features a great sword adjacent to the white staff of kingship. Above the sword, uniquely, is carved a small plaited cross, and this may be the relic from Jerusalem that tradition holds was gifted to Ranald.

The slab on the right may belong to Angus Òg (Angus the Young) who was a famous MacDonald clan chief, and led a fearsome phalanx of Islesmen at the Battle of Bannockburn in 1314. King Robert Bruce credited Angus with a decisive role in the battle, for which he was richly rewarded. This identification has recently been made from a reinterpretation of the inscription on this slab, which reads 'here lies the body of Angus, son of Lord Angus MacDonald of Islay'.

THE CROSSING

Above: The south crossing arch, with the nave beyond. Remodelled in the 1400s, the arches are extensively carved with floral, animal and human figures. This one features Adam and Eve.

The crossing is the junction of the four arms of the cross of the church. Its present form dates mainly from the mid-1400s. Only the north arch remains from the earlier crossing, though this was in-filled with a narrower opening during the later remodelling.

The massive two-storey tower above the crossing is reached by a steep spiral stair in the south–west corner. The original entrance to the stair was reinstated in 1910, having been blocked in the 1600s. The upper storey, housing the belfry and a pigeon-loft, is not accessible to visitors for safety reasons. It is lit by ornate windows that are best viewed from outside the church. The clock on the belfry window replaces a medieval clock, and the large bell was cast at Loughborough, England, in 1931.

Look out for carvings on the cross-arches and on the adjacent south aisle arcade. They show biblical subjects such as Adam and Eve, real and mythical animals, foliage patterns, depictions of contemporary life, including an armed rider and foot-soldier, and a scene showing four men preparing to slaughter a cow. Can you find the monkey?

AN AUTOGRAPH IN STONE

One of the masons left more of a trace of himself than was usual. An inscription on the south pier of the east crossing-arch, dating from about 1460, names the principal carver, who was perhaps also the master-mason: 'DONALDUS O BROLCHAN FECIT HOC OPUS' ('Donald O Brolchan made this work'). Donald seems to have been a member of an Irish stone-carving family – John Ó Brolchán carved the MacDougall Cross, which can be seen at Ardchattan Priory on the mainland.

Above: The tower, directly above the crossing.

Top: An elongated dog, wearing a collar, twists around to bite the bird perched on its tail.

Above: The slaughter of a cow in preparation for winter.

THE TRANSEPTS

The transepts lie to the north and south of the crossing, which separates the nave from the choir. Much of the stonework of the north transept belongs to the early 1200s. It is therefore the only substantial part of the original church to survive.

The north transept is late Romanesque in style, with Irish and Scandinavian influences, such as the small, wide-splayed windows and plain round-headed arches with mouldings at the base and head, one of which preserves its foliage decoration.

Two shallow chapels were created in the thickness of the east wall, each with its own altar. Between the chapels is a recess for a statue. Although only the feet remain, it is thought that a miracle-working statue of St Columba once stood here. It has now been recreated in contemporary wire form. The stained-glass image of the saint is by William Wilson and was added in 1965. As this transept was probably a focus for the cult of the saint, a display telling something of his life has been created here.

Above: The niche of the north transept held a statue, possibly of St Columba, but only its feet survive.

Left: The stone known as 'St Columba's Pillow'. The saint's biographer Adomnán tells how he used a stone for a pillow. This is in fact a grave marker of the 800s.

Far left: Marble effigies of the 8th Duke of Argyll, who initiated the abbey's restoration, and his wife Ina, lie in the south transept.

Left: A carved cross in the south transept commemorates the consecration of the abbey church.

Against the west wall is the reconstructed night stair, via which the monks shuffled down from their dormitory for the night-time services. Queen Elizabeth II gifted the oak screen which separates the transept from the crossing in 1956. The large rose window was inserted by the architect John Honeyman in 1904, but is now blocked externally by the reconstructed cloister buildings.

The so-called 'St Columba's Pillow' was found about 1km north of the abbey, and quickly became identified with the stone which traditionally marked St Columba's original burial place. There is no evidence to support this connection, and in reality this stone, carved about 200 years after Columba's death, would have marked a grave in an outlying cemetery.

The south transept was added in the 1400s and has received only minor alterations. The tracery of the three-light south window was renewed in 1875 on the model of the south presbytery window. There would originally have been space for two altars against the east wall but no evidence for their arrangement survives. A consecration cross can still be seen on the south side of the arch.

The effigies, made of Carrara marble, are those of the 8th Duke of Argyll (1823–1900) and his third wife Ina McNeil (d.1925). Only the duchess is actually buried here, the duke being interred at the family burial ground at Kilmun, Argyll.

THE SOUTH CHOIR AISLE

The south choir aisle was part of the alterations of the mid-1400s. The only feature to survive unchanged is a small window in the south wall at the east end. The tracery of the east window was restored in 1904 and the opening to its right was reconstructed as a three-light window at the same time. It may originally have been the sedilia – seating for priests officiating at a side altar here.

Remains of the large south-east extension of the 1200s lie underneath the current building. They were uncovered during the rebuilding of the church around 1910.

Left: The arcade dividing the choir from its south aisle, added during the 1400s.

THE CHOIR AND CHANCEL

Top: The modern communion table, made from Iona marble.

Above: The much-altered north wall of the choir, including the doorway into what is now the sacristy.

Just beyond the crossing is the choir, now with modern choir stalls marking the space where the Benedictine monks worshipped for three and a half centuries. Beyond this was the presbytery, occupying the east end of the church, where Mass was celebrated by their priests at the high altar.

This area was central to the monks' daily work of worship. For that reason, the east end was redesigned more than any other part through the centuries. The result is a rather confusing collection of features, although the essential sequence of developments can still be made out.

The original chancel was built around 1200. Its extent is indicated by the moulded sandstone string course that extends along the north wall for about 5m east from the crossing and then ends abruptly. The Torridonian limestone used in this phase contrasts with the granite used in later stages.

The double arch in the north wall is revealing. The base of the central column – almost 2m above the present floor – marks the former floor level of the choir. It was extended and raised around 1220–50. The two arches gave access to a north aisle.

Beneath the choir was a basement crypt, originally with a timber ceiling supported on a stone ledge. (Parts of the ledge can be seen below the north choir arcade.) The crypt may have been used to provide a more dramatic and secure home for Columba's relics, which by this time would have been removed from his ancient shrine chapel outside the church.

The crypt was removed during the 1400s. The raised choir was dismantled and the present floor level created, gaining impressive height for the east end. The earlier double arch was blocked, and the present ornate doorway formed, partly from what had been a door into the crypt. It gave access to a sacristy, where altar vessels, vestments and furnishings could be safely stored.

The new chancel at the east end was lit by three large windows with elaborate tracery, restored in 1874–5. This area was the presbytery, reserved for the clergy officiating at the celebration of the Mass. Near the south window are some of the finest additions of the 1400s: the piscina (a basin where the altar vessels were ritually rinsed), supported by two figures, now headless, and the beautifully carved, triple-seated sedilia (where the priests sat during parts of the Mass), whose decoration includes carvings of human heads. A socket in the floor near the altar shows where a lectern stood, used for scriptural readings.

The modern communion table is of Iona marble, set in a pavement of medieval sandstone slabs. The original marble altar was destroyed by souvenir-hunters in the 1700s.

To either side are the stone effigies of two of the most important abbots, clothed in their ecclesiastical vestments. The one on the south side is believed to be Abbot Dominic (1421–c.1465), who initiated the rebuilding of the 1400s, and the other is Abbot John MacKinnon (1467–c.1498), son of the clan chief.

A memorial in the floor, centrally placed in front of the position of the medieval high altar, indicates the burial place of a lay benefactor, perhaps a MacLean of Duart or even a MacDonald Lord of the Isles. This is exceptional, as the marble base slab (imported from Belgium) originally contained the effigy of a knight in European plate armour. Privileged burial in this especially sacred location was reserved for senior clerics and important patrons.

Top: An effigy thought to represent Abbot Dominic MacKenzie.

Above: A better-preserved effigy thought to belong to his successor, Abbot John MacKinnon.

THE CLOISTER

Above: The cloister walkway. Most of the piers are modern replacements, delicately carved by the sculptor Chris Hall over 30 years from 1967 to 1997. Look out for the two pairs which have survived from the medieval abbey.

The cloister at Iona is sited to the north of the abbey church. A cloister is a central court around which monastic communities in western Europe organised their domestic quarters. The covered walkways linked the church with the domestic buildings, but they also served as a place for quiet contemplation, and as part of the processional route into the abbey church.

The lean-to roof of the cloister is supported on a series of arches formed from pairs of columns. Although many original fragments survive and some were used in the 1958–9 restoration, most of the work you now see is modern. Many of the new column capitals are carved with bird and foliage designs.

The cloister was originally laid out in the 1200s, but like the abbey church it underwent changes in the 1400s. The corners were built up to give them greater strength and many of the openings were blocked up. The 1950s restoration was carried out to the designs of the architect I.G. Lindsay, following the original layout of the 1200s. Most of the buildings around the cloister date to this reconstruction. They are now actively used by the Iona Community and for that reason most are inaccessible to visitors.

However, visitors can normally access the chapter house, where the monks met daily to read a chapter from the Rule of St Benedict, a guide to monastic life, discuss business and confess sins; the original stone bench seats around the walls survive under modern covering.

In the north-east corner of the cloister is the day stair, which led up to the monks' dormitory on the upper floor of the east range, and in the north-west corner is the former refectory stair, now blocked but once quite an elaborate feature. The undercroft below the refectory now serves as the abbey gift shop.

DESCENT OF THE SPIRIT

In the centre of the cloister there might originally have been a 'tree of life', symbolic of all good things that come from God. The sculpture that now stands at the centre of the cloister is the work of the Lithuanian artist Jacques Lipchitz (1891–1973). It is called 'Descent of the Spirit' (1959), and it is inscribed (in French) 'Jacob Lipchitz, Jew, faithful to the religion of his ancestors, has made this Virgin for the better understanding of human beings on this earth so that the Spirit may prevail'.

Born in Druskieniki, Lithuania, Lipchitz moved to Paris in 1909 to study but fled to America in 1940 following the Nazi occupation. The sculpture was donated to Iona in 1959 and is one of three casts made of his 1948 work *Study for Nôtre-Dame de Liesse*. The other two are in Assy, France and New Harmony, Indiana, USA.

Below: 'Descent of the Spirit' at the centre of the cloister garden.

THE BAKEHOUSE, ABBOT'S HOUSE AND BISHOP'S HOUSE

As a centre of Christianity for nearly 1,500 years, Iona has vestiges of many abandoned buildings associated with the religious foundation.

Outside the western entrance of the cloister there is a low ruin, which is now laid out as a small garden. This was the site of the monastery's bakehouse and brewhouse, where bread and ale were produced to feed the community and guests. It is connected to the Sràid nam Marbh by a later medieval cobbled road. Excavations here have revealed remains of workshop buildings from the Columban monastery.

Continuing clockwise around the reconstructed west range, visitors pass the abbot's house, largely restored in 1956 and in use by the Iona Community. This would have been a grand residence for the head of the monastery, separate but attached to the cloister. Here, he could entertain important visitors to the island, and have space to attend to the administration of the abbey and its extensive lands.

Beyond the abbot's house to the north-east lie the ruins of the bishop's house, on the far side of Sruth a' Mhuillin, 'the mill burn'. This unfortified residence is thought to have been built for Bishop Neil Campbell in the 1630s, when the abbey church acted as the Cathedral of the Isles. It was described by early visitors as having a large living hall 'open to the roof', with a kitchen beyond on the ground floor and a bedchamber above.

Top: The wall footings are all that survive of the bakehouse to the west of the cloister. As a fire hazard, it was kept separate from the main abbey buildings.

Above: The surviving ruins of the bishop's house, probably built in the 1630s, when the abbey church was functioning as the Cathedral of the Isles.

THE ABBEY MUSEUM – IONA ACROSS TIME

Past the abbot's house, north-east of the cloister, stands a building that may once have been the monks' infirmary. Extensively reconstructed in the 1960s, it now serves as the Abbey Museum, telling the story of Scotland's most sacred place through its sculpture and other artefacts.

The museum takes visitors on a journey through key events in the history of this great monastery. Iona's sculpture is of great importance as the main surviving evidence of Columba's monastery, dating as far back as the 600s. Three reassembled high crosses are central to the story – a testament to the innovation and creativity of the early monastery. Later carvings reveal the continued importance of Iona in Gaelic political and spiritual life.

As well as the sculpture, you can discover some fascinating artefacts from excavations on Iona – many of which are on display for the first time – and a facsimile of the *Book of Kells*. This illustrated manuscript of the four Gospels is widely acknowledged as the finest of its kind in existence. It was created on Iona around 800, and helps tell the story of Iona as one of the greatest centres of scholarship in western Europe.

Above: This carved cross, dating from the 800s, shows that interaction with the Norse people was not limited to violent raids. The interlace pattern on the cross shows the influence of Scandinavian art. The carver ingeniously cut into this surface to reveal the glittering mica-schist within.

Below: The interior of the Abbey Museum. The current display was created in 2013, in a monastic building reconstructed in the 1960s. The abbey's infirmary may once have stood on this site.

FLOWERING OF FAITH

In the 700s and 800s, Iona Abbey was at the centre of a cultural revolution. The monks expressed their faith through the arts and learning, revealed to us today through their sculpture, metalwork and manuscripts.

The arrival of the first Christian monks and the conversion of the native peoples brought about tremendous changes in society. The new faith brought laws and writing, but the most tangible signs of the Christian revolution were new ways of commemoration – of the living and the dead.

Crosses of wood, and then of stone, were created to declare the sanctity of the place chosen by the revered Columba, and patrons were quick to pay for these as reflections of their own piety. Emerging beliefs required that the graves of the faithful be marked with a cross – the core symbol of Christianity. Many of these survive and some are displayed in the museum.

Marking the graves of the Christian dead with stone crosses is now conventional, but, amazingly, this practice may have been pioneered on Iona. The oldest grave marker here dates back to about 600.

Some of these early Christian stones were intended to stand upright, while others were recumbent – designed to lie flat over the grave of the deceased. The variety of cross forms is almost endless, and helps chart changes in political control, as well as the appearance of new peoples, such as the Vikings from the later 700s onwards. Most of these stones were originally placed in Reilig Odhrain, the abbey's adjoining cemetery. Some ancient slabs can still be seen nestling in its turf.

The early stones displayed here help present the archaeological evidence for a Columban golden age lasting into the 800s and beyond, the effects of which ripple through society to this day. The exhibition demonstrates how the translation (transfer) of Columba's relics from a simple grave to a shrine chapel, around 750, prompted this renaissance, previously unknown in what had been part of the pagan world.

Visitors can discover how the Iona monks produced sophisticated artistry in a variety of media, sharing a common set of symbols and designs, all to better glorify God, while emphasising the great importance of Iona and the relics of St Columba.

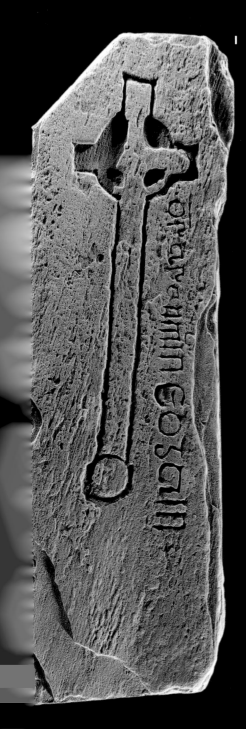

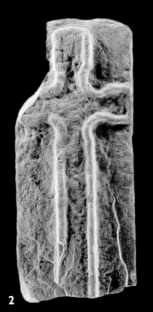

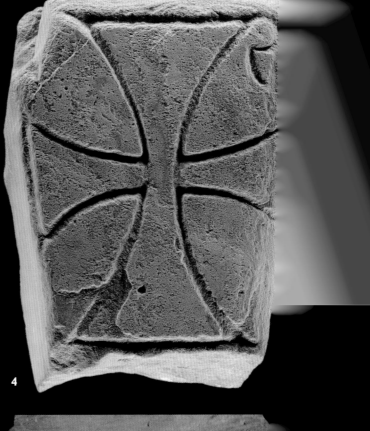

This page: Early Christian carved stones.
(1) A grave slab with ringed cross and elongated shaft.
The Gaelic inscription reads: 'A prayer for the soul
of Éogan'. (2) A recumbent slab decorated with a
Latin cross carved in low relief, with beaded edges
and rounded armpits. (3) A Latin cross with flowering
terminals, and a blade-shaped stem. This was re-used
for a later burial, overcut with a simple cross.
(4 and 5) An upright grave-marker, carved in early 600s.
A Latin inscription on the top face reads 'Lapis Echodi'
('The Stone of Echoid'). This might have marked the
grave of Echoid, king of Dal Riata (d. 629) whose
succession had been prophesised by Columba.

THE HIGH CROSSES

The high crosses were among the most sophisticated uses of the cross in Europe. Their carved imagery was designed to broadcast key messages of the Christian faith.

St John's Cross stands at the front of the display. This is the prototype ring-headed Celtic high cross: it was the first of its kind anywhere, carved more than 1,200 years ago. Its shape and decoration were entirely experimental, carved in hard stone imported by boat from Loch Sween in Argyll, 50 miles away.

The creation of St John's Cross was influenced by precious metal crosses which the monk-carvers knew from inside their church. This cross contains few figures, but instead is covered with complex patterns, all of which were rich in meaning for the educated Christian viewer.

The only creatures visible on the front of St John's Cross are lions (symbolic of the majesty of Christ) and snakes (symbolising wisdom and resurrection). The overall appearance is highly decorative, but everything has meaning – even the numbers associated with the carving. For example, three 'eggs' inside the circular nest bosses represent the Trinity, while five bosses arranged in a group evoke the five wounds suffered by Christ on the Cross. The lozenges that decorate the shaft are a symbol of divinity.

To its left is St Oran's Cross, which is slightly older, and to the right you can see St Matthew's Cross (about 1,100 years old). These had lain in pieces for centuries but have now been provided with special mounts, allowing them to stand once more in all their glory.

The decoration of these crosses was designed to be read with the movement of the sun during the day. Today, a 24-hour *son et lumière* sequence helps reveal how the carvings were meant to be understood.

This was a landscape dominated by the Christian Cross. We know that many others stood between the harbour and the abbey. But St John's, St Oran's and St Matthew's Crosses – along with St Martin's, which still stands in its original position in front of the church – are now the sole survivors from the early flowering of Christianity on the island.

Opposite: St John's Cross flanked by St Oran's Cross (left) and St Matthew's Cross (right). Their fragments have been reassembled and mounted to show how they would have looked when they stood upright.

GAELIC CHIEFS AND SWORDS FOR HIRE

Over the centuries, Iona played a vital role as the spiritual home of elite West Highland Gaelic society.

Among this sophisticated culture, with Christianity at its heart, the island was regarded as hallowed ground. Burial in its sacred soil was considered a gateway to the afterlife, and was therefore highly desirable.

Those with sufficient status and resources brought the bodies of their deceased loved ones to be laid to rest here, and also made arrangements for their own burial on the holy island. Elaborately carved stone slabs were laid over their graves, decorated with symbols, motifs and mesmerising patterns.

The museum's displays include a number of West Highland graveslabs, which commemorate the lives of great Gaelic leaders and swords for hire from the 1300s to the 1500s. Loyal in life and in death, they were buried in Reilig Odhrain, providing a posthumous honour guard to their MacDonald lords. The MacDonalds themselves were buried in St Oran's Chapel, their mausoleum at the centre of the graveyard. These slabs were laid flat over graves or else as covers of above-ground stone coffins.

Displayed here are all five of the surviving warrior effigies – one a MacKinnon, and the others MacLeans of Mull. The warrior effigies, and the majority of the other slabs in the cloister and in St Oran's, feature swords as a reflection of an elite military caste that emerged here in the medieval period.

Above: The five West Highland graveslabs now displayed in the museum were found in Reilig Odhrain. The effigies are carved in high relief, designed to honour these Gaelic leaders as noble warriors.

Opposite: A West Highland warlord equipped for battle.

These Hebridean warriors wore clothing designed to stand up to warfare in a harsh climate. Such a man wore a padded or quilted coat called an aketon, split for riding. This was made of leather stuffed with wool or straw and waterproofed with grease. His legs and feet were protected with armour, and equipped with spurs. He wore a mailed hood over his shoulders, and his head was protected by a conical steel helmet. Although these warriors are proudly depicted with swords, written records suggest their chief weapons were in fact axes, bows or spears.

By the early 1500s the Western Isles were supplying men to fight in Ireland as mercenaries in wars between rival kings. Records show that Hebridean chiefs could regularly muster a force of 6,000 to 7,000 men. These graveslabs and shields often feature their warships, which they rowed to the place where they would fight. Their command of the sea underpinned the power of this 'Kingdom of the Isles'.

PRIORESS ANNA MacLEAN

Although many of these graveslabs honour men of war, they are not the only ones commemorated. In the church you can see grave slabs of churchmen, and several of the stones in the cloister are dedicated to West Highland women. The gravestone of Anna MacLean (d.1543) was originally in the nunnery church, where she had been the last prioress. It was damaged in the 1800s when part of the church collapsed. However, earlier drawings show that the missing portion depicted the Virgin and Child. Her head is supported on a pillow held by two angels, and her lap dogs are at her waist nestling into her cloak.

Below left: Thomas Pennant's illustration of the 1770s shows that part of Prioress Anna's gravestone is now missing.

Below right: The surviving upper portion of Prioress Anna's gravestone.

MONASTIC MEDICINE

'For these sick let there be assigned a special room.'

In his Rule for monastic life, as well as setting aside a 'special room' for them, St Benedict wrote that 'above all things, care must be taken of the sick'. This was the basis of one of the main aspects of monastic hospitality: the provision of medical care. The abbey's infirmary would largely have been used to care for sick and elderly monks, but attending to pilgrims and other travellers would also have been important. As the educated elite in society, the clergy were among the few people to have access to medical knowledge and training; monastic libraries would have included medical texts.

Medieval medicine largely involved herbal remedies and simple surgeries. Evidence suggests that monks would have had access to a variety of plants. Excavation here at Iona in the 1970s revealed the presence of several plant species including ash, holly, nettle and honeysuckle.

These are known from later records to have had medicinal uses such as curing coughs or helping heal broken bones. Prior to the papal ban on blood-letting by clerics, surgeries would probably also have been performed, including trepanning (the cutting of a hole through the skull) and cataract removal.

The care provided would also have had a spiritual element. The belief that diseases were a result of sin was strong in medieval times, so no treatment of the body would be complete without attention paid to the patient's soul.

Pilgrims may have been particularly attracted to Iona due to its associations with St Columba's miraculous healing powers, particularly in relation to fractures and nosebleeds. He is also credited with one of the first recorded uses of St John's Wort, to cure a young boy whose mind had been disturbed by long nights alone tending cattle. Belief in his healing powers continued into the later medieval period at Dunkeld, where it was said that drinking water used to wash the saint's bones would provide protection from plague.

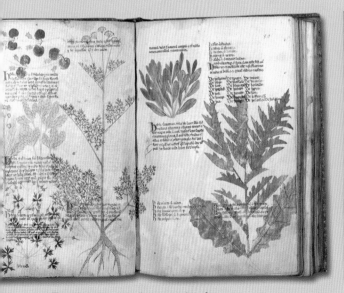

Top: A doctor attending to a patient, from a French manuscript produced in the 1300s.

Above: An Italian guide to medicinal herbs produced around 1340.

Above: A page from a French surgical manual dated around 1310 illustrates stories of saints above scenes depicting treatment of injured limbs.

SMALLER CHAPELS

As well as the abbey's main church, its precinct would have
contained a number of small chapels, which may have been used
by monks, and by pilgrims preparing for a visit to St Columba's shrine.
Two such chapels survive, in very contrasting states of repair.

THE MICHAEL CHAPEL

Close to the abbey museum sits a small chapel that was part of the
abbey in the early 1200s. The Michael Chapel may have served as the
Benedictine monks' temporary place of worship while they worked on
building the abbey's main church during the Benedictine colonisation
phase. It was rebuilt at a later date. The style of the windows suggests
that this work took place around 1500.

The whole chapel was fully restored in 1959 and it is from this date
that it becomes known by its present name. There is evidence for a chapel
or burial vault dedicated to St Michael on Iona and it is possible that it was
this building. The restoration was funded largely by donations from Africa;
the stalls and curved ceiling are of African timber.

Above left: The Michael
Chapel, the name now given
to a small chapel north-east
of the abbey church, originally
built in the early 1200s.

Above right: The Michael
Chapel's interior, refurbished
in 1959 using African timber.

Below: The ruins of
St Mary's Chapel.

ST MARY'S CHAPEL

A short distance south-east of the abbey church lies the ruined
St Mary's Chapel, which probably dates from around 1200.
It may have featured as a pilgrimage station.

THE VALLUM

The area around the monastic settlement was enclosed by a boundary or vallum, a deep ditch bordered by a bank formed from the upturned earth.

The best-preserved stretch of the vallum lies a short distance north-west of the abbey. To reach it, follow the road north, past the Iona Community's shop and over the mill burn. The vallum's steep contours are clearly visible to the left of the road, rising to an impressive height. Even in its weathered state, the drop from the top of the bank to the bottom of the ditch is over 4m.

The vallum marked the dividing line between the secular world and the spiritual realm inhabited by Columba and his successors. However, it is not only the product of Columba's monastery. Radio-carbon dating has suggested that portions of it date to a much earlier period, perhaps as early as the 1st century AD.

This suggests that Columba may have chosen the site for practical reasons: the existing earthwork would have provided a ready-made boundary.

He may also have wanted to associate himself with a site that was already sacred or important, much as the builders of the later medieval abbey did by building on Columba's monastery.

The vallum once enclosed the whole monastery – an area of around 8 hectares. The enclosure was modified throughout the life of Columba's monastery, and was possibly fully developed during the 700s. By this time the monks had created a double enclosure, bisected by the mill burn.

The early abbey was approached via the Sràid nam Marbh, which entered the outer precinct near where the St Columba Hotel now stands. This outer precinct contained a number of burial grounds, the first of which was Reilig Odhrain, with an earlier version of St Oran's Chapel. This route and the entrances would have been marked by standing crosses.

After passing St Oran's visitors would enter the inner enclosure, with a heightened sense of anticipation as they approached the spiritual core of Columba's monastery – the high crosses, the tiny shrine chapel, and the early church.

Above: Columba's monastery as it may have looked in the late 700s. The church stands on the spot now occupied by the abbey church, overlooked by Tòrr an Aba. Chapels, high crosses and ancillary buildings are enclosed within the vallum, which encircles the entire complex.

INVESTIGATING THE INNER ENTRANCE DITCH

A length of the inner ditch was excavated in 1979 at its terminal with the causeway for the Sràid nam Marbh, just north of St Oran's Chapel. It was 6m wide by 3m deep, and had been partially filled with refuse by the monks soon after it was originally dug in the early 600s.

Most exciting of all was the discovery of preserved organic objects in the waterlogged lower fills. Numerous worn leather shoes had been thrown away here, along with substantial carpenter's debris from discarded parts of wooden buildings, along with evidence of a wood turner making bowls for the monks' porridge.

The best preserved and most substantial early monastic building was found just inside this ditch. This was a circular timber round house 18m in diameter – much larger than any other domestic building found in an early monastery in Britain and Ireland.

This could even have been the *magna domus* – communal living quarters – described by Adomnán in his biography of Columba. It stood just to the east of the Sràid nam Marbh, where the mill-stone base of a lost high cross was found. Could this be one of the crosses erected to commemorate significant events in the life of the saint?

Adomnán's account, written about 690, describes how Columba went to bless a barn on the last day of his life. 'After this the saint made his way back to the monastery. Where he rested halfway, a cross was later set up, fixed in a mill-stone. It can be seen today at the roadside.'

Top: An archaeological excavation of the ditch in 1979.

Centre: Part of the vallum as it survives today.

Above: A mill-stone found just to the east of Sràid nam Marbh, and probably once used as the base for a cross. This may relate to the tradition that a cross was erected in a mill-stone at a place where Columba stopped to rest on the last day of his life.

REILIG ODHRAIN

Just south of the abbey lies the Reilig Odhrain burial ground, where many of Iona's carved cross slabs and gravestones were found. Legend identifies this as the burial place of early Scottish kings, where famous monarchs such as Macbeth are believed to be buried.

Reilig Odhrain was consecrated as the monastic burial ground as soon as Columba founded his monastery. By around 1200 this became the favoured place of burial of the clansmen loyal to the MacDonald Lords of the Isles, including MacKinnons, MacLeans and MacLeods.

However, despite Reilig Odhrain's iconic status as the burial place of many early Scottish kings, experts now doubt this due to lack of written or archaeological evidence.

But it is certainly the case that *Ri Innse Gall* ('Kings of the Isles') were buried here, or in the nearby chapel. These were Gaelic-speaking Hebridean chieftains. They included:

- Godred, died 1187.
- Ranald, son of Somerled, founder of the later abbey and nunnery, died about 1210.
- Hakon, died 1230.

Some of these may have been buried in the three tiny funerary chapels which once stood in the cemetery, which were recorded as being in ruins by the 1700s (see also page 63).

More recently, the Labour leader and member of the Iona Community, John Smith (d.1994), was buried in the northern extension to the cemetery.

Above: Graves in Reilig Odhrain, with St Oran's Chapel left and the abbey church beyond.

Right: The gravestone of John Smith, former Labour leader, one of the most prominent burials of recent years.

ST ORAN'S CHAPEL

The chapel standing in Reilig Odhrain is Iona's oldest intact structure. It probably dates from the 1100s.

St Oran's Chapel was probably built as a dynastic mausoleum by Somerled, the self-styled 'King of the Isles', who died in 1164. It may well have replaced an older chapel on the same site. Irish influence can be seen in both the architecture and the decorative doorway of this fine but simple building.

Some of their undisturbed tombs still survive. The most honoured positions were around the high altar, and it is possible that Somerled and his son Ranald lay under slabs to the south and north of the altar respectively. There is a central slab, apparently in its original position, just inside the door. This is very worn by footfall, but it does feature the sword and white staff insignia presented to new Lords of the Isles.

Early records show that this was the burial place of John, 1st Lord of the Isles and Donald, 2nd Lord of the Isles. The son and grandson of Angus Òg – the MacDonald chief who had played such an important role at the Battle of Bannockburn – they died in 1387 and 1421 respectively. Donald was 'laid in the same grave as his father' on the south side of the church.

Top: The tomb recess within St Oran's Chapel was probably installed around 1500.

Above: An attractive Romanesque building, St Oran's Chapel probably pre-dates the Benedictines' first church by several decades, and much of it survives unaltered.

There is a fine canopied mural tomb in the south wall, and there was once another to its left (now lost). These were probably constructed by John MacDonald II, the last Lord of the Isles, for his predecessors and himself, before his forfeiture in 1493. It was probably then appropriated by Abbot John MacKinnon for his own family use.

Although much of the structure is original, it has received some repairs. The granite quoins – the external corners – at the south-west and south-east angles date to the mid-1800s. The slate roof, plaster, whitewash and sandstone altar are part of the 1957 restoration.

DID YOU KNOW...

When he visited Iona in the late 1700s, Thomas Pennant (right) was told a local legend about St Oran. When Columba created Reilig Odhrain, he needed to consecrate it with the burial of a faithful Christian soul. His follower Oran offered to die immediately to satisfy this need. Fortunately for St Oran, this is likely to be a fictional tale.

MacLean's Cross

MacLean's Cross stands beside the road between the abbey and the nunnery. This fine cross was erected around 1500, at a point where the ancient Sràid nam Marbh met a track leading up from Port Rònain ('St Ronan's Port'), where the modern pier is today.

It is likely that this tall and very slender cross stood on the pilgrim trail, providing a focal point for pilgrims to stop and pray on their way to the abbey. It was commissioned, as an act of piety and commemoration, by the chief of the MacLeans of Duart in the late 1400s. It was probably carved on Iona by one of the sculptors responsible for making graveslabs.

Carved from a single stone slab more than 3m high, it stands in its original socket-slab on a modern base. The west-facing side was the front, and this is where the faithful would have stood, facing east, contemplating the figure of the crucified Christ in the centre of the cross head. Above him, the upper cross arm is decorated with a lily, a symbol of the Virgin Mary.

A panel at the foot of the back contains a very worn mounted warrior, together with a now illegible Latin inscription, perhaps recording the patron's name.

Below: The two faces of MacLean's Cross. The west face (left) shows the Crucifixion, while the east face is decorated with ornately interwoven floral and animal motifs.

THE PARISH CHURCH AND MANSE

The present parish church and the former manse stand near MacLean's Cross, across the field to the west. Though the church is still in use, the manse now serves as the island's heritage centre.

The parish church was built in 1828 to a standard design of the Scottish civil engineer Thomas Telford. This was one of the so-called Parliamentary Churches, built across the Highlands following an 1824 Act of Parliament, which supported the construction of over 40 new churches in the Highlands and Islands.

The manse, to the south of the church, is also of Telford's design, but the central portion was raised in the early 1900s. Its ground floor now houses the Iona Heritage Centre. Run by local residents, the centre hosts a display of photographs, artefacts and records telling the story of the island's recent history, focusing on the lifestyle and work of the residents. An admission charge is payable.

Below: The church (left) and manse (right) designed by Thomas Telford and built in the 1820s.

ST RONAN'S CHAPEL

The chapel lying just north of the nunnery is Teampull Rònain, or St Ronan's Chapel. It served as the parish church of Iona from around 1200 until the Reformation of 1560. Aside from the abbey's short-lived revival as Cathedral of the Isles, the island had no place of worship until the present kirk was built. It was restored in 1923 and again in 1993.

This plain building is surprisingly small, given the population of the island. However, medieval churches did not have seating, so more people could be accommodated.

Excavations beneath the floor in 1992 revealed traces of a smaller, earlier chapel, perhaps dating to the 700s. Beneath were burials of even earlier date. These show that there was a lay population on the island at the time when Columba's monastery was thriving. All of the later burials were found to be female, which suggests this area was reserved for the burial of women.

Left: Teampull Rònain, close to the nunnery, acted as the island's parish church for more than 350 years.

THE NUNNERY OF ST MARY THE VIRGIN

The Augustinian nunnery was founded around 1200 by Ranald, King of the Isles. Although much of it is now ruined, it is one of the best preserved nunneries in Britain.

Augustinian nunneries were common in Ireland, and it is likely that many of Iona's first nuns were Irish. Like their male counterparts in the abbey, the nuns followed a life of contemplation and prayer. The sisters lived off the income from the modest estates they were granted, chiefly in central Mull, as well as on Iona and adjacent islands. They augmented their funds by giving hospitality to female pilgrims to Iona, and received the parish incomes from a number of Hebridean churches.

Above: The nunnery from the south. Although most of the cloister lies in ruins, parts of the church are still upstanding.

Above: One of four silver gilt spoons found as part of a hoard in the nunnery church, and probably dating from the 1200s. The precious metals suggest that at this time the nunnery was quite wealthy.

We know little about the nuns as individuals, and it seems they were not held in high regard in the 1400s, probably because they were often caught in the crossfire of land disputes. However, lay women of noble birth were brought to the nunnery for burial from far and wide, a tradition that continued until long after the nunnery ceased to function at the Reformation of 1560.

An elaborate double-ended graveslab (see page 33), was badly damaged when the roof of the chancel collapsed in 1830. It was carved as a memorial to Prioress Anna MacLean, who died in 1543. Plans to restore the nunnery were drawn up in 1917, but repairs were only carried out in the north chapel and the sacristy.

Top left: The surviving rib-vaulted ceiling in the small chapel at the north-east of the nunnery church. The design of the window shows Irish influence.

Above: A delicately embossed gold fillet, also part of the hoard discovered in the nunnery church. It would have been used to secure a veil, and provides further evidence of wealth.

THE LAYOUT OF THE NUNNERY

Like most religious houses, the nunnery was laid out around a square cloister, with the church along the north side, oriented to face the east, and the other buildings arranged along the east, south and west sides.

The nunnery church was originally constructed in the 1200s. It consists of a nave with an aisle of three bays on the north side, a small chapel at the east end of the aisle, and a chancel, originally separated from the nave by a wooden screen. It is little altered from its original design and may reflect something of the original appearance of the abbey church.

Like the abbey, the nunnery has a simple design. The north chapel has an Irish-style triangular-headed window and a rib-vaulted ceiling. This is the only intact part of the church. The chancel also had a rib-vaulted ceiling, a rare feature in West Highland medieval architecture.

The capitals of the nave arcade and the corbels that supported a timber gallery at the west end of the nave (inserted around 1500) still preserve some of the fine carvings that once decorated the church. The arcade in the nave was probably blocked up during renovations in the 1400s.

Above: The nunnery as it may have looked when complete and in use. The church is shown at the left of the cloister. The detached building at the far right is Teampull Rònain.

To the south of the church is the cloister, laid out as a garden in the early 1900s. Only the foundations of the cloister arcade now remain, but surviving fragments show that it was beautifully decorated. Clues in the surviving masonry suggest that the nunnery was enlarged in the 1400s. The original cloister may have been smaller than the 14m square that exists today.

The west range of the cloister has been lost completely (it lies under the modern road). It may have contained guest accommodation and cellars. The footings of the east range survive. It contained three rooms at ground level, including the chapter house, with stone benches around the walls. The nuns' dormitory was probably on the upper floor.

The south range is the best preserved. It consisted of a large refectory where the nuns took their meals. After the Reformation, the east part of the refectory was adapted for domestic use by the insertion of an upper floor. The exterior roadside wall of the refectory contains a worn carving of a sheela-na-gig (a carving of a naked woman), placed above the middle window to ward off evil.

There would have been ancillary buildings in the precinct adjacent to the cloister, including kitchens, an infirmary, a guest range, a bakehouse, a brewhouse, a malthouse, a dovecote, a barn, and a granary.

Top left: The nunnery church, viewed from the south range of the cloister.

Top right: Two of the decorated corbels surviving on the south wall of the nave. They would once have supported a timber gallery at the west end of the church.

AROUND THE ISLAND

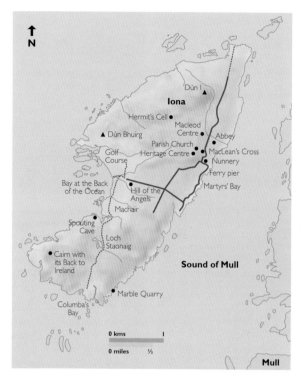

PORT NAM MAIRTEAR ('MARTYRS' BAY)

The road leading south from Baile Mor, the main village, leads past the war memorial to Port nam Mairtear. This is said to be where the bodies of kings and clan chiefs were landed before being borne along Sràid nam Marbh to Reilig Odhrain and the abbey. More recently, Clyde 'puffers' beached here, bringing essential supplies to the island.

Top left: Map of Iona.

Above: Columba's Bay from the west.

Top centre and top right: Some of the surviving machinery at the marble quarry; the machair from the south.

PORT A' CHURAICH ('BAY OF THE CURRAGH')

This pretty bay at the south end of the island is the site where Columba is said to have landed on his arrival at Iona. The Gaelic name refers to Columba's use of a traditional skin boat.

Getting to the bay is quite a hike but well worth the effort. At the shoreline you can collect small translucent pearls of green marble, known as 'St Columba's tears', reputed to provide protection to those travelling over water.

MARBLE QUARRY

The abandoned marble quarry lies near Druim Dhùghaill on the south-east coast of the island, not far from Port a' Churaich.

The quarry may have earlier origins, but the first machinery was installed around 1790. Founded by John Campbell, 5th Duke of Argyll, in partnership with the industrialist William Cadell and the Swiss geologist Rudolf Raspe, it may have been part of an effort to stimulate the economy and discourage islanders from leaving to find jobs elsewhere. It proved too expensive to transport the marble off the island and the quarry closed after only a few years.

The duke also tried to establish a spinning school around this time, but it too closed after a few years. The quarry reopened from 1907 until 1915. The visible remains date from this last period of activity. The badly rusted winch survives, together with a cutting frame, a water tank and the gas engine.

NATURAL HERITAGE

Aside from its cultural importance, Iona has a geological history distinct from its neighbours. Its natural heritage, partly shaped by its human residents, is also unique.

Although Iona lies close to Mull, its geology is quite different. Mull was mainly formed by volcanic action some 60 million years ago, but Iona is geologically much older. It is formed mainly from Lewisian gneiss, part of a plate of rock extending throughout the Outer Hebrides. Most of this rock was formed about 2,700 million years ago, and it is among the oldest in Europe.

Grey and common seals are present around the coasts of Mull and Iona in internationally important numbers. Further offshore, minke whales, killer whales, basking sharks, porpoises and dolphins can sometimes be seen. These sea mammals feed on the abundant plankton, fish, crabs and oysters surrounding the islands, which also support a thriving fishing industry.

There are many birds around Iona, including the red-throated diver, kittiwake, Atlantic puffin, goldeneye, and the recently re-introduced white-tailed sea eagle.

In particular, the Hebrides have become the last British stronghold of the corncrake. This secretive bird is extremely difficult to see due to its well camouflaged colouring and preference for long vegetation. It seeks early cover in yellow flag iris beds until the hayfields grow tall enough.

Although it is rarely seen, it is characteristically noisy, with its distinctive 'creaking' call. Long ago, people believed corncrakes spent the winter under the ice; however, we now know that they migrate from Africa, arriving in May. Numbers are now on the increase.

Historically, birds would have contributed to the diet of the island's inhabitants. Young puffins, known as guga, were a particular favourite and were salted and stored for consumption in the winter.

Although snakes are abundant on Mull, they are not found on Iona. According to Adomnán's account, Columba miraculously rendered their venom harmless on the island.

The heath and coastal grassland, known as the machair, is colourful with flowering plants in spring and summer. Flowers to be found around the coast include bedstraw, harebell, autumn hawkbit, wild thyme, eyebright, wild carrot, buttercup, vetch and bird's foot trefoil. Cotton grass, marsh marigolds and wild iris grow in wet areas. Ling, bell heather and cross-leaved heath can be found in upland areas.

Some plants undoubtedly owe their presence to the medieval monks. For example, deadly nightshade is still found on the island. Although poisonous, it was cultivated for its medicinal properties. Trees were cleared by early settlers, and there is little tree cover to this day.

Above, left to right: A grey seal, one of the species commonly seen in the Sound of Iona; a corncrake; yellow flag, the corncrake's favoured haunt until the hay is tall enough to hide it.

THE HISTORY OF IONA

This page: A statue of
St Columba at Bishop's House,
built in 1894 at the end of the
main street of Baile Mòr.

Iona has a long and rich history. One of Scotland's smallest inhabited islands, it has a cultural and historical significance out of all proportion to its size. First colonised in prehistoric times, it became famous in the early-medieval period as the site of St Columba's monastery and drew many pilgrims to its shores.

The Columban community survived numerous Viking attacks around 800, although this was followed by an exodus of some brethren, taking with them the most important relics.

Monastic life was reinvigorated around 1200, when the monastery was transformed into an abbey for the Benedictines, one of the new reformed orders coming from Europe. They were fiercely opposed by the Columban church in Ireland: the Irish chronicles record that Irish clerics attacked and 'pulled down' the new monastery in 1204. However, the Benedictines flourished under the patronage of the Lords of the Isles until eventually falling victim to the Protestant Reformation of 1560.

Despite this loss, Iona has continued to attract pilgrims and tourists over the centuries. In the late 1800s, the process of restoration was begun by the Duke of Argyll, and it was continued by the Iona Community in the 20th century. Today the abbey is once again home to a vibrant faith community.

THE PREHISTORY OF IONA

Iona is a small island, only three miles long and one mile wide
at its narrowest point. Its economic resources were always limited,
but a reasonable living could always be made from the land,
supplemented from the sea. Settlement can be traced back
at least until the Bronze Age.

There is fertile land along the north-east of the island, where Columba founded
his monastery. There is also a strip of good farmland across the middle of the island,
stretching to the machair, the sandy grasslands fringing Camus Cul an t-Saimh,
the Bay at the Back of the Ocean. In these areas, cereal crops could be grown
and cattle pastured. Seaweed, readily available on the island, made a good
fertiliser for the fields and could also be used as fuel.

The oldest surviving prehistoric site on the island is the small burial cairn
Blàr Buidhe. Although it has not been excavated using modern techniques,
comparison with mainland sites suggests that it is Bronze Age,
about 3,000 years old.

Above: A cairn on Dùn I, at 101m (330ft)
the highest point on the island.

VENI VIDI IONA

The Graeco-Roman historian Plutarch (left) records a Roman sea-borne expedition around Scotland, which followed Agricola's subjugation of the Caledonii at the Battle of Mons Graupius in AD 83. The navigators had been ordered by Emperor Domitian to carry out reconnaissance of the 'islands of Britain'. They 'sailed to the nearest of these' occupied by a small number of holy men held sacred by 'the Britons'.

The description suggests the Inner Hebrides and possibly Iona. Archaeological evidence shows that this was definitely not a remote uninhabited island. It may well have already had a long history as a hallowed place, and this could have influenced Columba's decision to make this his headquarters.

There is only one Iron Age fort on Iona, not on Dùn I, the 'Hill of Iona', the highest on the island, but on Dùn Bhuirg, the 'Hill of the Fort', at the north end of the machair.

The fort had a stone wall along the landward side of the hill (the steep seaward side needed no extra defence) and small round stone houses. Excavations have produced pottery and glass beads dating from the 1st century BC to the 3rd century AD, but the hill may have been occupied for longer. The fort was uninhabited by the time Columba arrived.

Right: Epidote-rich gneiss of a kind often found on the island. It is sometimes mistaken for Iona marble, which is white with yellow or green serpentine and was used for the communion table in the abbey church.

TIMELINE

c.1000 BC

A BURIAL takes place at Blàr Buidhe cairn (left), the oldest evidence of human habitation on the island.

c.100 BC

A HILL FORT is established some time during the Iron Age at Dùn Bhuirg (left), near the island's west coast.

COLUMBA'S ARRIVAL

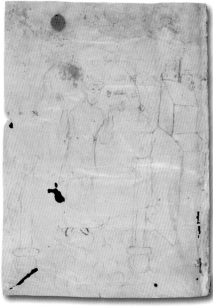

When Columba arrived in 563, Argyll and its neighbouring islands were part of Dál Riata. This was a small kingdom incorporating roughly what is now Argyll and the Inner Hebrides, closely related to the Irish kindreds in Antrim.

On first arriving in the region, Columba stayed with Conall mac Comgall, one of the sub-kings of Argyll. Later, he moved to Iona, and it is possible that Conall gifted the island to Columba and his monks.

Iona would have been an attractive location for Columba and his followers, not least because it may already have been a hallowed place. It also bordered a number of territories on the edge of Dál Riata and Pictland. The British kingdom of Strathclyde lay to the south, and Saxon Northumbria was not far away. Iona's influence reached all these places.

Top: 'The Coming of Columba' by the Scottish Victorian artist William McTaggart imagines the arrival of the holy man's boat.

Left: The earliest surviving image of Columba, found in a copy of Adomnán's *Life of Columba* at the monastery of St Gallen in Switzerland. It dates from about 875.

Although it now seems remote, in Columba's time Iona was located on an ocean highway, making it an excellent base for travel between Ireland and Scotland and the numerous islands of the west.

According to tradition, Columba and his 12 companions landed at Port a' Churaich, the Port of the Curragh, at the south end of the island.

The curragh was a light but sturdy vessel with a wooden framework, over which animal hides were stretched and sewn. The boat was then greased to make it watertight.

At Columba's Bay today, there are a number of cairns of different sizes in the pebble shingle, well back from the sea. These are thought to be the work of pilgrims over the centuries, commemorating both Columba's arrival and their own.

Left: Columba in stained glass above the music loft in the abbey church.

521/2

563

COLUMBA
is born into the ruling Uí Néill family in County Donegal in the northern part of Ireland.

COLUMBA
arrives on Iona with a small group of followers and establishes his monastery.

COLUMBA – THE GREATEST SAINT IN AN AGE OF SAINTS

Columba is the first historical figure in Scotland whose life is reliably documented. We know that he came from Irish aristocratic stock, and we know a good deal about his life's achievements.

In 521 or 522, a son then named Crimthann was born into a branch of the powerful Uí Néill family. They were overlords of much of northern Ireland in the early-medieval period, dominant in what is now County Donegal.

This man is better known to us today as Columba or Colum Cille ('Dove of the Church'). He seems to have been destined for the church from an early age. He was fostered with a priest as a child, and in the 540s studied at Leinster and under Uinniau (Finnian), possibly in his seminary at Clonard, Co Meath.

This excellent education equipped Columba as a priest, poet, musician, scribe and scholar, and he was already an important and influential monk even before he left Ireland. He had founded monasteries, and was immersed in a culture of the written word. He seems to have become embroiled in political controversy, however, and he may have left Ireland in voluntary exile to focus on his life as 'soldier of God'.

Columba's aristocratic background immediately made him worthy of respect and hospitality from kings and nobles who shared his kindred and culture. His band of 12 followers included other noblemen.

Contrary to tradition, he probably undertook little missionary activity. The large-scale conversions sometimes attributed to him were probably achieved by Columban and other missions after his death. This was not his primary interest: his monastery was a place of withdrawal, not a pastoral centre. He represented the pinnacle of Christian virtues, as an example for others to emulate.

Above: An illustration of the saint in Manus O'Donnell's *Life of Columba* (c.1550).

Left: A curragh – a simple boat made from animal hide stretched over a wooden frame. A vessel of this kind was probably used by Columba to travel to Iona in 563.

His mission at Iona was clear – to create the perfect monastery as an image of the heavenly city of Jerusalem. But to achieve this he also had to be a shrewd politician, a hard-nosed negotiator and a gifted administrator.

Columba founded several monasteries aside from Iona. They included Hinba (possibly Colonsay), Mag Luinge on Tiree, another near Loch Awe, one on the unidentified Elena Insula, along with Durrow and Derry in Ireland. He thus became the head of a monastic federation that would long outlive him.

His greatest achievement was to establish and lead this network of churches and monasteries on both sides of the North Channel, with an incomparable reputation for holiness in his own lifetime.

As well as travelling throughout the isles, he regularly travelled closer to home, and in Ireland. He also visited the Picts on the mainland, probably in the southern Highlands. But he was generally resident on Iona.

On the island, Columba lived the life of an ideal monk. Adomnán writes that he occupied his time copying manuscripts, praying or meditating and leading his monks in worship and daily work.

Columba gave practical and spiritual advice to lay visitors as well as to his community, and imposed penances on offenders. In the last weeks of his life he is said to have blessed each part of his beloved island, its crops, livestock and people, before his death in the half-lit church of his monastery on 9 June 597.

Right: An artist's impression of Columba's burial on Iona in 597.

597

COLUMBA dies in his church, at the heart of the monastery he founded on Iona.

634

KING OSWALD OF NORTHUMBRIA gifts the tidal island of Lindisfarne, off the coast of north-east England, as the location for an Ionan monastery.

COLUMBA'S MONASTERY

Above: A monastic scriptorium, or writing hut, of a kind that would have been used by Columba and his successors on Iona.

Very little of Columba's own monastery is now visible. Parts of the vallum still survive, though some of it may be earlier or later than Columba's time. Our best source of information is Adomnán, augmented by the results of archaeological investigations.

The most important building was of course the small, wooden church, the remains of which probably lie beneath the present abbey church. However, there would also have been accommodation and facilities for the monks and guests.

Another important building is likely to have been the scriptorium. It is not clear when this developed at Iona, but manuscript production was certainly a major activity by Adomnán's time, and probably earlier.

In common with many buildings of the period, the structures of Columba's monastery are likely to have been made of wood and thatch. There are written references to fetching timber and gathering reeds, and archaeologists have found the remains of wooden buildings. Traces of large-scale metalworking have also been found, together with waste from glass-making, leather working and woodworking. The high crosses and graveslabs show that stone carving was a regular activity.

For the large community of monks to live here comfortably, this had to be a well-equipped and well organised farming community. They created a mixed livestock economy on the island, led by dairying for the production of butter and cheese. Deer, cattle, pigs, sheep, seals and fish (including deep-sea fish) all featured on the menu. The arable fields were on the machair on the west shore.

But the monks were not self-sufficient, and depended on food tributes coming from lands they controlled in the region. Some of their craft production may have funded their access to exotic commodities required for liturgical use, such as wine, oil and pigments, traded from southern France, possibly via the Dál Riatan royal capital at Dunadd in mainland Argyll.

Sandbanks and fast tidal currents make the Sound of Iona treacherous to navigate, although this would have been a necessary journey for the inhabitants, relying on Mull and the adjacent Scottish mainland for supplies, especially timber and good stone for building and carving.

Top: Fragments of window glass found at Iona, possibly dating from the 600s. They may even have been peered through by Abbot Adomnán.

Above left: A glass rod with a delicate helix design, made to decorate glassware on the island in the 700s.

Above right: A glass bead decorated with spirals and a herringbone pattern. It was found druing the excavations of 1959.

'A GOOD AND WISE MAN': COLUMBA'S BIOGRAPHER

Bede's description of Adomnán indicates the high regard in which he was held. As his near-contemporary, the Northumbrian monk and scholar was admiring of the abbot's accomplishments.

Adomnán was abbot for 25 years in the late 600s, and, aside from Columba, he was Iona's most important leader. He is perhaps best remembered for his biography *Vita Sancti Columbae* ('Life of Saint Columba'), written in the 690s. This is one of the best sources of information we have for life in the monastery and about Columba himself, though it probably tells us more about Adomnán's own time than it does about Columba's.

It focuses on his miracles, divided into three books:

• Miracles of prophesy and predictions of distant events.

• Miracles of power – for example, raising the dead and changing the weather, opening the gates of Pictish King Brude's fortress simply using the sign of the Cross, drawing water from a rock (like Moses) for a baptism, and answering prayers for help and protection.

• Miracles of heavenly apparitions and heavenly light, showing how closely connected he was to God. Countless angels sent down to carry home his soul; angels and holy lights at his grave.

Adomnán also wrote a much-copied book about the places associated with Christ's Passion, *De Locis Sanctis* and established the *Lex Innocentium* ('Law of the Innocents') in 697. This law aimed to protect women, children and clergy in times of war. It was supported by religious and secular leaders in Ireland and Scotland and was renewed several times in the following century.

Adomnán also acted as a diplomat, travelling to the Northumbrian king Aldfrith (a former monk of Iona) to secure the release of Irish hostages who had been taken in a raid in 684 by his predecessor, King Ecgfrith.

Above: In his account of Columba's visit to Loch Ness, Adomnán describes how the saint baptised a Pictish man named Emchath as he lay on his deathbed.

690s

ADOMNÁN, ABBOT OF IONA writes his *Life of St Columba*, still an invaluable source of information about Iona.

c.800

THE BOOK OF KELLS is created at the monastery on Iona. It is later moved to Kells in Ireland to preserve it from Viking raids.

THE MONASTERY AFTER COLUMBA

The monastery flourished after Columba's death – indeed its influence expanded, supported by the reputation of its founder.

Columba died in 597, but his monks continued to develop the monastery, and also founded several daughter houses elsewhere in Britain. Most famously, in 634 the Northumbrian king Oswald invited Ionan monks to found a monastery at Lindisfarne.

Adomnán's Law of the Innocents was renewed in Ireland and his relics were displayed there. The monastic rites and leadership of Iona was respected throughout much of Scotland and Ireland for centuries to come. In the 700s at least two Irish kings retired to live out their last days at the monastery.

The creative output of Iona at this time was groundbreaking, and established the monastery as a beacon of civilisation and theological scholarship within western Europe. The high crosses remain as evidence of exquisite stone carving. It is also possible that some of the finest metalwork of the time was produced on Iona, but the precious jewelled containers have been lost, presumably in the Viking raids.

One area where we know the Columban monks excelled was in the production of illuminated manuscripts. This particular area of expertise culminated in the finest example of the era – the *Book of Kells*.

LIFE AFTER DEATH

The greatest treasures of Columba's monastery were not the gold and jewellery gifted by wealthy patrons, but the bones of the saint. The opening of Columba's grave is thought to have prompted an outpouring of spiritual creativity in the production of reliquary containers and high crosses here on Iona.

Adomnán tells us that at the time of writing his Life of Columba in the 690s, the saint still rested in his grave 'frequently visited by the holy angels and illuminated by heavenly light'. All this changed around 750 when the momentous action was taken of opening the grave to access the bones and other powerful relics. We know this because in 753 his bones were taken on circuit around Ireland, to promulgate laws and consecrate churches. This also provides a date by which the first shrine chapel was built here, at the termination of the Sràid nam Marbh processional way.

To allow Columba's sacred remains to travel, they would have been placed within a richly decorated reliquary chest, while other reliquaries would have been produced for his personal possessions – secondary relics.

This would have been the greatest religious event in Britain and Ireland of its time. Kings and nobles of Ireland and Pictland would have queued up to offer pious gifts of enormous value – and this in turn paid for reliquaries, the shrine chapel and crosses. One possible sponsor is the Pictish king Óengus son of Fergus (d.761), who had taken control of Dál Riata in the 740s.

Top: The Monymusk Reliquary, which was once thought to be associated with Columba. Similar, church-shaped containers may have been used to carry his relics.

Right: The arm reliquary of St Patrick, made from gold and decorated with gems. We know that a similar container was commissioned for St Columba's hand by Donald, Lord of the Isles, in the 1400s.

Left: The 'Cathach of St Columba', now held in Dublin, may be the oldest surviving Irish manuscript. Some people think this version of the Psalms may have been written by Columba on Iona.

THE BOOK OF KELLS

The *Book of Kells* was the supreme creation of its age, produced on Iona around 800. It contains the complete Gospels of Matthew, Mark and Luke and a portion of John's Gospel, and was drawn from the Vulgate – a Latin version of the Bible completed around 400.

Known as the great Gospel book of St Columba, the *Book of Kells* was created by a small team of highly skilled monks in the scriptorium at Iona, possibly to commemorate the 200th anniversary of the death of St Columba in 597.

The quality of artistry, design and complex iconography is superb. The production of this luxury Gospel book required enormous resources, and like the high crosses, it must have been paid for by a king. Only a few senior clergy would have been able to decipher the convoluted display script, and so it would only have graced the altar on special occasions.

Soon after the book was completed, it was removed from Iona to protect it from the Vikings. Thereafter it was housed in a newly founded Columban monastery at Kells in Ireland, along with other sacred relics. It is now displayed at Trinity College, Dublin.

The identification of the *Book of Kells* as a product of Iona has been reinforced by the results of the latest research. Examining the manuscript alongside a handful of reliquary fragments now in foreign museums, we can see a common symbolic decorative language shared between these exquisite objects.

Similar motifs are clearly present on the high crosses of Iona. They include symbolic snake-and-boss decoration, together with lions, which represent Christ as the Lion of Judah. The breakthrough in this research was the rediscovery of a tiny, backward-looking bronze lion, originally excavated at the abbey in 1959. Its resemblance to lions in the *Book of Kells* is startling.

Top: A brightly decorated page from the *Book of Kells* shows figures representing Matthew, Mark, Luke and John.

Left: Recurring motifs in early-Christian art from this region suggest that they were all the work of closely linked craftsmen. (1) A lion looking over its shoulder from the *Book of Kells* (top) is strikingly similar to a sinuous pair of animals carved on the top part of St Oran's Cross (2) and a tiny cast bronze lion also found at Iona (3).

THE VIKINGS

Above: An illustration from a medieval manuscript shows Vikings preparing to disembark in England.

Iona's location, ideal for Columba's monastery, made it vulnerable to a new threat that appeared off the coasts of Britain in the 790s. Viking raiders were beginning to seek out opportunities for plunder.

As skilled seafarers, the Vikings had no difficulty navigating to the northern and western islands of what is now Scotland. Monasteries, being undefended and possessing valuable treasures, made attractive targets.

Iona suffered several Viking attacks in quick succession, the first in 795 (just two years after its daughter house at Lindisfarne had suffered), followed by one in 802 and another in 806, the latter resulting in the loss of 68 lives.

Fear of Viking devastation led to the removal of Iona's treasures, including the bulk of St Columba's relics, eventually divided between Dunkeld and Kells. One of the worst raids was in 825, when Abbot Blathmac and his monks were tortured and killed for refusing to reveal the hiding place of Columba's relics. A poem written soon afterwards indicates that the shrine chest was covered with gold and silver. These were the martyrs of Martyrs' Bay, near the ferry port.

'The violent cursed host came rushing through the open building, threatening cruel perils to the blessed men; and after slaying the rest with mad savagery, they approached Blathmac to compel him to give up the precious metals wherein lie the holy bones of St Columba.'

Walafrid Strabo, Abbot of Reichenau, Germany

During the 800s and 900s the abbacy of Iona and Kells was held jointly, although the power and influence of Iona was on the wane. This was not just due to Viking attacks, but was more to do with the shift of political power to the east, and the emergence of a more centralised Scottish kingdom.

By 815 a new royal church was founded at Dunkeld in Perthshire, housing some of Columba's relics, and this became a new cult focus for pilgrimage and later, a great medieval cathedral.

Above right: The silver and gold bezel of a ring buried at the abbey around 990, perhaps to hide it from Viking raiders.

Right: The head of a pin found on the island in December 2013, and thought to date from the Viking era.

Despite continued Viking attacks and the loss of Columba's relics, the island monastery survived; indeed it seems to have flourished. There are more graveslabs at Iona from the Viking Age than from the earlier period. By around 900, Vikings had settled in the Hebrides and embraced Christianity, adopting the still mighty Columba as their patron saint.

The Abbey Museum holds several gravestones recording the deaths of Christian Vikings. One runic inscription translates as: 'Kali the son of Olvir laid this stone over his brother Fugl.' One Norse king of Dublin, Olaf Sihtricsson, even retired to Iona in 980 to end his days quietly.

But old habits die hard. Danish Vikings who had settled in Dublin raided Iona on Christmas night 986, when they knew that rich treasures would be on the altars for the festive Mass. The abbot and 15 monks were murdered at the White Strand of the Monks (Tra' Ban nam Manach) at north end of the island.

An incredible insight into this event was gained when workmen digging drains near the abbot's house in the 1950s found a hoard of 363 silver coins and other precious objects. The coins may have been deposited under the floor of the monastic treasury just before 986, a family treasure concealed for safekeeping. Although its hiding place was entirely effective, sadly the owners never returned to claim their riches.

Above: A small bronze head representing Christ or a saint. Found at the abbey and dating from the 900s, it may have formed part of a figure, or perhaps the head of a decorative pin.

DID YOU KNOW. . .

Much of the Vikings' success was down to their carefully designed longships and their superb seamanship. The Lords of the Isles, with much Viking blood in their veins, also controlled the waterways of western Scotland, and the design of their birlinn (right) was based on earlier Viking designs.

795

FIRST VIKING RAID on Iona. Further raids are to follow in 802, 806 and 825. Eventually, holy relics and other valuables are sent away from the island for safekeeping.

c.815

DUNKELD is founded to house Columba's relics. The site becomes a focus for pilgrimage and later, a major medieval cathedral. Its seal (left) depicts Columba.

SOMERLED AND THE LORDS OF THE ISLES

The islands off Scotland's west coast were beyond the effective control of either the Norwegian or the Scottish crown. This provided an opportunity for a dynasty of warlike chiefs to take power, eventually titled the Lords of the Isles – a kingdom within a kingdom.

From around 1100, Iona and much of the western seaboard was nominally under the control of the Norwegian king. However, he was too remote to govern the region. Nor could the king of Scots effectively exercise power so far from his own power base in the eastern mainland.

Right: An effigy thought to represent Gilbride MacKinnon, chieftain of one of the powerful clans, and a member of the Islesmen's council.

From the mid-1100s, Somerled, a Gaelic–Norse warlord known as 'King of the Isles' (Ri Innse Gall), took control of an area that stretched from Kintyre to the Outer Hebrides. His descendants, the MacDougalls of Lorn, the MacDonalds of Islay, and the MacRuairis of Garmoran, dominated the region for many years, ruling from such mighty castles as Dunstaffnage, near Oban.

The descendants of Somerled's son Ranald founded the powerful southern MacDonald clan. They expanded their influence through their support of Robert the Bruce during the Wars of Independence in the early 1300s, and through skilful political manoeuvring thereafter. From 1336 the MacDonalds assumed the title 'Lords of the Isles'.

These lords were different from their counterparts in the rest of Scotland. They spoke Gaelic and pursued their own foreign policies. But they were similar in other ways. They built castles, issued charters and patronised the great monastic orders coming from Europe. In 1164, Somerled himself invited a reforming Irish abbot to Iona. About 1200, his son Ranald brought Benedictine monks and Augustinian nuns to Iona.

Top: King Robert I (the Bruce), who received support from the Islesmen during the wars against England in the early 1300s.

Above: Robert's son and successor David II. During his reign the MacDonald chiefs adopted the title 'Lord of the Isles'.

Right: Dunstaffnage Castle near Oban, a stronghold of the MacDougall clan.

The Lords of the Isles governed with the advice of a council, which included the abbot of Iona. Many of these great chiefs, among them MacKinnons, MacLeans and MacLeods, were brought to Iona for burial in Reilig Odhrain.

St Oran's Chapel, probably built for Somerled himself, remained the burial place of the Lords of the Isles until the late 1400s. They remained generous benefactors to the abbey throughout; Earl Donald (d.1421) had a precious shrine made for a part of St Columba's hand. But in 1493 the lordship, weakened by family feuds and years of wrangling with the Stewart kings, was finally declared forfeit by James IV. The title Lord of the Isles was thereafter bestowed on the heir to the Scottish throne (Prince Charles holds this title today).

The forfeiture of the lordship probably also had a detrimental impact on Iona craftsmen, who lost the patronage of the wealthy lords who had previously chosen to be buried and commemorated on the island.

ROYAL BURIALS?

Reilig Odhrain has iconic status as the legendary burial place of early Scottish kings. One of those said to have been buried here is Cinead son of Alpín (Kenneth mac Alpin, d.858), often viewed as the king who unified the Picts and the Scots. Others include Mac Bethad (Macbeth, d.1057), made famous by Shakespeare, and Donald Bán (d.1097), who also appears in Shakespeare's play. However, there is not much evidence to back up this tradition.

It may have arisen through a misunderstanding of the records, or perhaps through royal propaganda. Alexander I may have sought to create a distinction between the 'old' line of kings, ending with his uncle Donald Bán, with Iona as their mausoleum, and the 'new' dynasty beginning with Alexander's parents Malcolm and Margaret, buried at Dunfermline.

Above: Finlaggan, on the Isle of Islay, the chief seat of the MacDonald Lords of the Isles.

c.985

A HOARD OF COINS is buried on Iona, probably to protect it from Viking raids. As well as more than 360 Anglo-Saxon coins it includes the bezel of a finger ring (see p.60).

1164

SOMERLED, 'KING OF THE ISLES' invites a reforming Irish abbot to Iona, but dies the same year.

BENEDICTINE MONKS AND AUGUSTINIAN NUNS

By the late 1100s, a Columban community still existed on Iona, but it had fallen into decline. In 1200, Ranald, Lord of the Isles, invited Benedictine monks to revitalise Columba's monastery under his patronage. At the same time, he established a community of Augustinian nuns.

The first Benedictine community in Scotland is thought to have been established at Dunfermline, Fife, soon after 1070. Iona was the last to be founded. The Benedictines were known as the 'black monks' because they wore black habits.

At the same time Ranald established a community of Augustinian nuns. Nunneries of this order were popular in Ireland, but they were rare in Scotland, with one here and another at Perth.

The Augustinian nuns too wore black habits, and their nunnery church on Iona was locally called *an eaglais dhubh*, 'the black church'. The abbey church was simply known as *an eaglais mhor*, 'the great church'.

The introduction of these new forms of monasticism does not mean that Columba had fallen out of favour. Indeed, the Lords of the Isles seem to have maintained a special devotion to the saint and documents still referred to the monastery of 'St Columba of Iona'.

When choosing a site for the incoming religious regimes, Ranald would have chosen Iona as the region's premier spiritual location. After all, he needed the help of the most powerful saint, and of the best monks, to ensure the rapid entry into heaven of himself, his family, and his royal line, in return for his investment. Older traditions were still maintained, and Cellach, the last Columban abbot, seamlessly adapted to his new role as the first Benedictine abbot.

The new foundation was gifted extensive lands, chiefly in Mull, Colonsay, Canna and Coll, to ensure that the monks could live comfortably on Iona. Rents were paid in kind – oatmeal, cheese and salt beef. Unlike the early monks, the Benedictines' focus was largely on the work of worship.

Above: The cloister walkway as it may have looked following the remodelling of the abbey in the mid-1400s.

THE DAILY ROUND

The Rule of St Benedict was essentially a user's guide to the monastic life. It provided a considerable amount of structure to a monk's (or nun's) daily activities – and this was particularly evident in the area of prayer. Monastic foundations were largely intended to act as beacons of prayer in a sinful world and monks were required to attend eight daily services. These would begin very early in the morning and continue throughout the day (and night). Each service would include prayers, psalms, hymns and readings.

These offices were interspersed with celebrations of the Mass and other services particular to the time of year, or to the importance of a certain day in the calendar. After the first Mass of the day, the community met in a room adjacent to their church, called the chapter house, where a chapter from their rule was read (hence its name) and where they confessed their sins and conducted business.

Between services there was time for spiritual, intellectual and manual activity – St Benedict's Rule required monks to engage in physical labour. The gardens had to be tended, books written, meals made, guests looked after, and patients in the infirmary cared for.

Above: An illustration from a manuscript produced at Nîmes in southern France in the 1120s shows St Benedict delivering his Rule to his followers.

In 1204 the building site which would become the new monastery on Iona was attacked and badly damaged by a force led by two Irish bishops along with abbots of Derry and Armagh. The Columban clergy in Ireland would not accept the loss of its connections and influence at Columba's own foundation.

The raid was initially successful, but the Benedictine brethren were soon restored to Iona, and from then on the abbey played no part in the religious organisation of the Irish Church, which felt it had been abandoned by Columba.

Left: An illustration from a French manuscript of around 1400 shows nuns worshipping in choir stalls.

c.1200

BENEDICTINE MONKS

invited to establish a community on Iona, replacing the Columban establishment.

c.1200

AUGUSTINIAN NUNS

invited to establish a community on Iona, a short distance to the south of the Benedictine house.

PILGRIMAGE

It is difficult to overstate the importance of pilgrimage to Iona. The ability to attract many pilgrims was an important sign of status for the monastery and also a valuable source of income.

The shrine of St Columba was the final destination for pilgrims, at the end of a long and hard journey. After reaching Iona, pilgrims would probably have followed a trail around the island before finally reaching the shrine. This route would have incorporated outlying crosses, chapels, burial grounds, hermitages and holy sites associated with St Columba's many miracles.

Pilgrims probably landed at the Port nam Mairtear ('Martyrs' Bay) or Port a' Churaich (St Columba's Bay) before progressing around the island. They came for a variety of reasons: some for healing, some in response to an oath, but chiefly to salve their souls of sin. More worldly motives may also have stimulated pilgrimage, though – it would have been one of the few opportunities most people had to travel to new places.

The holy relics representing Columba were not exclusively fragments of his human remains, but included items thought to have been owned by him. Even when most of the relics were removed to safeguard them from Viking raids, Iona still attracted pilgrims, indicating that the place itself was still considered important. The Benedictines continued to encourage pilgrims, although the only relic recorded on the island was the 'hand of St Columba'.

The original focus for medieval pilgrims was probably in the north transept of the abbey church, where there had been a statue of the saint. This area may have been set aside for the reception of pilgrims before the east end of the church was remodelled to provide a more fitting space behind the high altar. This remodelling also included large aisles on the north and south of the choir, allowing a one-way system for the pilgrims, to manage their progression around the shrine. This may indicate a growth in the number of pilgrims coming to venerate the saint.

Above: An artist's impression of medieval pilgrims arriving at the abbey.

Below: A pilgrim's badge showing the martyrdom of St Andrew. Probably dating from the 1300s, it would have been sewn to a pilgrim's hat or clothing by rings at the corners, three of which have been lost.

Efforts to attract pilgrims continued into the 1400s. In 1428 Abbot Dominic petitioned the Pope to grant an indulgence of three years off purgatory to all pilgrims visiting Iona on Columba's feast day (9 June). The abbot was no doubt seeking to boost the abbey's income to help pay for the new building work that was needed in the church.

Well before the Protestant Reformation of 1560, Iona became part of the estates of the Campbells of Argyll. In 1499 John Campbell, Bishop of the Isles, was appointed commendator (administrator and effective owner) of the abbey. Monastic life continued, albeit in a reduced form. The Reformation had only limited impact – two of the recent bishop-commendators had been Protestant sympathisers, and by this time the number of monks was small. Some monks were allowed to live out their days quietly in the secularised abbey buildings.

Above: St James the Great depicted as a pilgrim in a French manuscript of about 1325. His hat, staff, satchel and badges all indicate pilgrimage.

1266

THE TREATY OF PERTH brings an end to territorial conflict between Norway and Scotland, and Iona is ceded to the realm of the Scottish king, Alexander III (left).

1428

ABBOT DOMINIC petitions Pope Martin V (left) for a special indulgence to be bestowed on pilgrims visiting Iona on St Columba's feast day.

THE AFTERLIFE OF THE ABBEY

'That man is little to be envied, whose patriotism would not gain force upon the plain of Marathon, or whose piety would not grow warmer among the ruins of Iona.'

Samuel Johnson, *A Journey to the Western Islands of Scotland*, 1775

Top right: Dr Samuel Johnson, who famously visited the Hebrides in 1773.

Top left: Johnson's travelling companion, the Scottish man of letters James Boswell.

Above: A watercolour of the abbey painted in 1792.

The Reformation of 1560 brought an end to monasteries all over Scotland. However, Iona did not immediately lose its importance.

It was on Iona in 1609 that a meeting took place which culminated in the Statutes of Iona (see below). It has been suggested that the proceedings of this meeting gained weight thanks to the continued sanctity of the island.

In the 1630s, Charles I attempted to restore the abbey church as the Cathedral of the Isles, and work began on the east end of the building. His efforts were short-lived. The king's religious policies, including his use of bishops, were unpopular in Presbyterian Scotland. Bishops were finally and permanently removed from the Church of Scotland in 1690 and hope of reviving the abbey church disappeared.

It was at this point that Iona embarked on a new life as a tourist destination. Martin Martin, Scottish explorer and author, came to Iona in the 1690s and described the abbey as 'anciently a seminary of learning, famous for the severe discipline and sanctity of Columbus'.

The English writer Samuel Johnson and his Scottish companion James Boswell followed his trail a century later. Dr Johnson, who tended to take a fairly dim view of the Scots, declared, 'We were now treading that illustrious Island, which was once the luminary of the Caledonian regions, whence savage clans and roving barbarians derived the benefits of knowledge and the blessings of religion.'

THE STATUTES OF IONA

The Statutes of Iona were drawn up in an attempt by James VI (left) to bring a greater degree of political control to the Gaelic-speaking Highlands and Islands of Scotland. Among their most significant provisions was that of forcing clan chiefs to send their heirs to the Lowlands to be educated in English. The statutes were designed to bring Highland culture more into line with that of the rest of Scotland, and played a part in weakening the bonds between chiefs and their people, making the relationship a much more commercial one.

RESTORATION

'… I have come to the conclusion that it would be well for me to transfer my right of property and ownership in the said buildings to a public trust in connection with the Established Church of Scotland …'

George Campbell, 8th Duke of Argyll, Deed of Trust, 1899
(Displayed in the south transept of the abbey church)

After more than two centuries of neglect, the abbey buildings had deteriorated badly. It was only at the end of the 1800s that work began to reverse the decline.

By 1874 the abbey had fallen into ruin, apart from the east end of the church and tower. As a result, the 8th Duke of Argyll, who owned the entire island, commissioned the celebrated architect, Robert Rowand Anderson, to consolidate the ruins. In 1899 the Duke transferred ownership of the abbey, Reilig Odhrain and the nunnery to the newly established Iona Cathedral Trust, which was committed to restoring the church for public worship.

Despite some misgivings on the part of several architectural historians, the restoration was completed under the direction of Thomas Ross, John Honeyman, and P. MacGregor Chalmers, all leading architects of their day. On 14 July 1905 the first service was held in the partially restored church. Work on the nave was completed in 1910.

Restoration of the monastic buildings began in 1938 after the establishment of the Iona Community (see page 70). It used designs by Ian G. Lindsay, and was completed in 1965 with the construction of an entirely new west range to the cloister.

Much of the island of Iona was bought from the trustees of the Argyll Estate in 1979 by the Fraser Foundation and given to the nation in the care of the National Trust for Scotland. MacLean's Cross had long been in State care but in 2000 the Iona Cathedral Trust gave the abbey, Reilig Odhrain, St Ronan's Church and the nunnery into the care of Historic Scotland.

Top left: George Campbell, 8th Duke of Argyll.

Above: Two photographs of the abbey church taken in the late 1800s, shortly before work began to restore it.

1560

THE REFORMATION
led by John Knox (left) and others establishes Protestantism as the official religion of Scotland, bringing an end to monasticism.

1630s

CHARLES I
launches a scheme to restore the abbey as a Cathedral of the Isles, but the project soon falters.

THE IONA COMMUNITY

Today the restored abbey church and cloister are in daily and lively use by the Iona Community. An ecumenical movement, the Community seeks 'new ways to touch the hearts of all'.

The Iona Community was founded in 1938 by the Rev George F. MacLeod of Govan Old Parish Church in Glasgow. It was an innovative initiative, originally designed to prepare young ministers for the rigours of working in deprived inner-city areas. With this in mind, MacLeod brought together craftsmen from his parish and trainee ministers to work on rebuilding the abbey, a project that lasted several decades.

The Iona Community is a dispersed worldwide ecumenical Christian community working for peace and social justice, rebuilding of community, and the renewal of worship. Members are drawn from all the major Christian traditions and have a wide range of backgrounds. They include both lay and ordained men and women of various ages and occupations.

The Community now leads morning and evening worship, and in the summer months a short early-afternoon service for day visitors. In addition, visitors will often hear musicians or choirs practising, or see the sacristan preparing the church for the worship of God.

The Iona Community welcomes guests each week, from Easter to October. Forty-five visitors (as well as staff) can stay in the abbey cloister, and a similar number at the MacLeod Centre nearby. There is also an outdoor adventure centre at Camas, on Mull. Guests are invited to share in work and worship, and to discuss issues of the day, or learn about the environment of the Hebrides or the history of Iona. One day each week is spent on a pilgrimage round the island.

As well as its island centres, the Community has a mainland base in Glasgow, where the leader is based and from where the Community's programme of youth development work is co-ordinated.

Above: Members of the Iona Community at work on restoring the abbey buildings in 1939.

MODERN TIMES

'Whisky, which is a rarity here, is in profusion at marriages and has a wonderful effect upon the singers and dancers. A funeral is not considered decent or respectable without "a drop". Ministers have been trying a great deal to put a stop to it but have failed so far.'

Extract from 'Life in Iona (by one who lives there)'
Oban Times, 11 July 1885

If Columba were to return to Iona today, he would probably find the essentials of life much the same as they were in his own time.

The Columban (and later Benedictine) monks worked the land, welcomed visitors and worshipped God. Today, the islanders still work their crofts and offer hospitality to the many visitors who come each year, either for spiritual reasons or out of interest in Iona and its history. Meanwhile the Iona Community once again makes the abbey a place of vibrant Christian worship.

Above: Baile Mòr around 1890.

Above: Baile Mòr in modern times.

ARCHAEOLOGY

Iona has long been inhabited, but much of the evidence of its occupation and use can no longer be seen above the ground. This can only be revealed and understood through the work of archaeologists, working either as part of a research project or in advance of building work. Numerous investigations have been carried out over the years and have added substantially to our understanding of the island's history. However, there is much still to be discovered and understood about this important place.

Right: A bronze pin found during excavations on a housing site in 2012.

0 10 20 30 40 50 60 70 80mm

1938

REV GEORGE F. MACLEOD founds the Iona Community, and puts trainee ministers to work on rebuilding the abbey.

1952

HER MAJESTY THE QUEEN visits Iona with the Duke of Edinburgh, just six months after ascending to the throne.

Iona is one of many Historic Scotland properties on and around Scotland's west coast, a selection of which is shown below.

DUNSTAFFNAGE CASTLE

From this mighty Argyll power base, built around 1220, the MacDougalls of Lorn dominated the frontier between Scottish and Norwegian territory.

BONAWE HISTORIC IRON FURNACE

The most complete cold-blast furnace in Britain, Bonawe was established in 1753 to take advantage of local water power and charcoal, and survives largely intact.

ARDCHATTAN PRIORY

A monastery of the Valliscaulian order, founded around 1230, probably by Duncan MacDougall, owner of Dunstaffnage. Parts were incorporated into Ardchattan House around 1600.

KILCHURN CASTLE

Spectacularly sited on Loch Awe, Kilchurn's square tower was built as a noble residence around 1450 and greatly expanded in 1693 to include Scotland's first purpose-built barracks.

Near Dunbeg off the A85	By Taynuilt off the A85	On Loch Etive, off the A828	At the NE end of Loch Awe; access under railway viaduct
Open all year (Closed Thu and Fri, Nov–Mar)	Open summer only	Open access	Open summer only
01631 562465	01866 822432	01631 562465 (Dunstaffnage)	01631 562465 (Dunstaffnage)
Approx 3 miles from Oban	Approx. 10 miles from Oban	Approx. 7 miles from Oban	Approx. 10 miles from Oban

For more information on all Historic Scotland sites, visit www.historic-scotland.gov.uk
To order tickets and a wide range of gifts, visit www.historic-scotland.gov.uk/shop

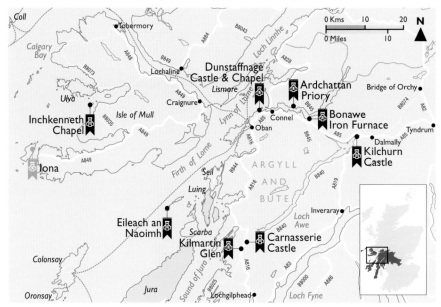

Key to facilities

Car parking	P
Bus parking	
Toilets	
Strong footwear recommended	
Interpretive display	
Visitor centre	
Shop	
Picnic area	
Tea/coffee making facilities	
Accessible by public transport	
No dogs	
Closed at lunchtime	